EDWARDIANA FOR COLLECTORS

EDWARDIANA
FOR COLLECTORS

Therle Hughes

LONDON : G. BELL & SONS : 1977

PRINTED IN GREAT BRITAIN BY
EBENEZER BAYLIS & SON LTD
THE TRINITY PRESS, WORCESTER, AND LONDON

ISBN 0 7135 1884 7

Contents

List of Plates

LINE DRAWINGS

Preface

This period is so rich in fascinating material that here I can do no more than suggest pointers for future research. It is so near yet so remote that my constantly recurring problem has been to avoid the more generally familiar while sharing my own pleasure in very many details already threatened with wrong ascription or total oblivion.

Many fellow enthusiasts deserve my thanks for their help. In particular I am grateful to Miss Alison Kelly for speeding my work by contributing Chapters 11 and 12. Others have taken time and trouble to produce illustrations worthy of the period's magnificent materials and expert workmanship, notably the outstanding photographer Mr Percy Hennell. Many busy museum authorities have proved extremely helpful, especially at Birmingham, Bradford, Brierley Hill and Stourbridge, Cheltenham, Leicester and London's Victoria and Albert Museum. I have been privileged to browse through many old records, notably those of Messrs Heal and Son and Mappin and Webb and as always I have found the owners of such treasures extraordinarily welcoming. But especially it has been my delight throughout the preparation of this book just to sit back and listen to those who by their own participation, influence and discriminating choice made so much of Edwardiana infinitely enjoyable.

THERLE HUGHES

I

Introduction

How remarkable it is, the brilliance of the Edwardian image, this half-memory filled with rainbow colour and lilting melody, sun-baked days and glittering nights. *Of course* the rich were self-esteeming, self-indulged, with inborn elegance jostled by self-made-and-proud-of-it swagger, but they were seldom idle; the poor were still abused yet astonishingly buoyant. And all were extraordinarily involved with each other throughout the whole complex structure of society, from 'Good Old Teddie' to 'cockney sparrer'. All had their dreams: 'there were visions about', and none brighter than those of the men and women who provided the substance of this book, the artists and designers, manufacturers and craftsmen who expressed them with a uniquely Edwardian panache.

All the foundations had been laid already, of course, in late Victorian days, by men as different and enduring as William Morris and Christopher Dresser. The aesthetic movement's medieval fairy tale escapism had become the Edwardian decorative arts' vernacular, along with the arts and crafts guild concept of working designer-craftsmen, the enjoyment of materials for their sensuous beauty regardless of price, Japanese and Celtic fantasies and the organic forms of anti-historical *art nouveau*. But from the Victorians, too, lingered resistance to such changes, shared with earlier periods of transition, even to the extent of repeating many features of late Elizabethan, late Stuart and late Georgian domestic furnishings. Among Edwardians, indeed, the mood was intensified. It was as if a growing sense of foreboding had to be smothered by the sheer pomposity of safe neo-classic ornament, the costliness of elegant costume, the strident artificiality of county family house party and workaday variety show.

Throughout the range of their interests collectors find many reflections of the traditional architect's arcaded, massive-chimneyed family seat with its Jacobean or Louis XVI furnishings, but as many more where the harmony of design and ornament point inexorably to the sparse, orderly geometry of the modern movement. And for those

Walter Crane drawing published in Grimm's Household Stories. *Engraved by* Joseph Swain.

who revel in this pattern of contrasting moods, collectable items abound.

Not only are they 'period' in every telling detail but they meet the shrewd collector's criteria of interesting design, attractive material and fine workmanship.

This was an age of freelance designers, under the vigilant eye of *The Studio*. But architecture was still the basic discipline for men who might earn a living from a dozen inter-related crafts. Walter Crane, for example, in 1909 was described as a designer of mural decoration, plaster and gesso relief work, stained glass, metal work, tiles and pottery, wallpapers and textiles, and a worker in oils, water colours and tempera, gesso, black-and-white and coloured book design, calligraphy and illumination.

Long ago Ruskin had envisaged our cities in 'endless perspectives of black [iron] skeleton and blinding square', countered by Christopher Dresser's declaration that 'rounded lines . . . generally produce feebleness of effect, whereas angularity . . . gives vigour and life'. A fairer summary of the new approach perhaps would be F. L. Griggs's description of Ernest Gimson's home: 'Nothing was there but for use and comfort, and all without any sort of make-believe.' But, above all, this was a period when the challenge word was *New*, and how remarkably young were many of the men who shaped it. In 1900, for example, even authoritative C. R. Ashbee was only 37, Ernest Gimson, Henry Wilson and W. Shand-Kydd 36, Baillie Scott 35, C. R. Mackintosh 32, Ambrose Heal 28, Ann Macbeth 25, Bernard Cuzner 23.

Other writers have filled in the background scene, the sensation-fraught town life and a countryside desolation, confounded by our garden cities that led the world, the joyous discovery of cycling and the motor car, even the naïveté of those famous posters and saucy postcards. Working conditions were often appalling and the real standard of living was falling: a commentator in 1907 saw 'no money anywhere except at Christie's. Within those enchanted portals the influences of high bank rate and low consols seem powerless'. Yet nothing could check a sense of progress. *The Queen*, 'the Lady's Newspaper', might still play Lady Bountiful, begging ten shillings to find new boots for a deserving family. But the same columns carried reports of women factory inspectors. Gossipy descriptions of magnificent titled ladies promoting Christmas bazaars drew attention to an extraordinary range of classes in home arts and industries up and down the country, fostered by state and local enthusiasm. Girls might still submit to the cult of the mature woman but fine clothes could never daunt the ladies' rifle clubs, the mixed hockey, the winter

"GIVE US A BITE."

Drawing by Phil May, who developed his modern 'brilliantly parsimonious' style to meet the defective printing conditions he encountered in Australia. From The Studio, *Winter number 1900–1.*

sports. Like their genial new king, gentlemen emerged from their clubs to assert their benevolent authority but their wives now revelled in the entertaining luxury of the department store, the tranquillity of the tearoom, the fun of the bargain basement. Debenham & Freebody's, for example, was magnificently extended in 1907, while reformist taste—and many a forward-looking designer—found refuge in Liberty's or Heal's. The Army and Navy Stores, like the Civil Service Stores, still had the kudos of being exclusive to its members. As for children, one look at the toys is enough to confirm the magic of those days, the days of Beatrix Potter, Arthur Rackham and *Little Folks*, of Wendy house and pedal car, of Titania's Palace and model planes. Potter's wheel and Harbutt's plasticine served the junior arts and crafts enthusiast, and eventually colourful Permodelle.

Collectors find emphatically Edwardian items pre-dating the arrival of the new century and post-dating 1914 (Registration numbers often help with dating a pattern—beginning at 351202 in 1900). But it is more important here to note the extent of change within a brief period that could be entranced alike by Yeats and Kipling and Elgar. Women's costume highlighted the changing image. The admired early Edwardian was a dreamy, swan-like figurehead of a mature woman, a willing captive in gossamer lace and crowned by the 'honey-coloured ramparts' of her hair. Her close-draped skirt emphasized slender waist and shapely hips, flaring out around her ankles in an absurdity of frills. Before the end of the period she was a straight-backed willowy figure, the tailor-made line ending perhaps in the cramping hobbled hem of extreme fashion or the slit tango skirt excused as voguishly Japanese. The wide 'Merry Widow' hat was her last flaunting indulgence, but even this was challenged by the close-fitting toque. Custom dictated great use of white and black as a background to the period's sensuous colour schemes, cool or fiery as the favourite opal and conservatory orchid. But here again nothing could suppress the assertive colour-jangles of the last frantic years of opulent fantasy illustrated by the exotic Russian ballet and Parisian Paul Poiret.

All this and so much more reached its zenith in Edwardian days, to be caught and held in isolation between the eruptive arrival of the new century and the holocaust of war. Now collectors with golden memories must share it quickly with those who will soon regard its artefacts indiscriminately as antiques.

Already too many have forgotten how excitingly the colour glowed in enamels, stained glass, beaten copper and lustrous china at the period's beginning, and how refreshing appeared the slim, rectilinear image towards its end. My purpose here is to set out at least a few

of the facts as they were presented to everyday Edwardians, whether by mass market industrialist or reformist designer-craftsman, by traditionalist or trend-setter, by professional or amateur. And to do so while still there are some who remember, and care, and are certain that those were the finest days to be alive.

2

Furniture

SCOTLAND's huge Kinloch Castle on Rhum was created in 1902 in the traditional splendour of castellated turrets, with antlered heads around the galleried hall, lion and leopard skins on the crimson drawing room carpet. Yet in the same decade the *Art Journal* declared this to be the century of the Flat Furniture designer, meeting current necessities of little space, portability and a dirty atmosphere. Such contrasts typify this fascinating period. Today students are surprised not so much by the variety of this furniture as by its instant declaration of its era.

Leaders of design found inspiration in the clean lines introduced by Victorian engineers working in iron, steel and reinforced concrete; for refreshing grace they looked again at late Victorian Oriental imports such as Liberty textiles. Both furniture designers and their clients needed only time to accept the ideas that gradually clarified into the twentieth century's modern movement. But meanwhile the furniture demands of Edwardian prestige clients ranged in style from the fully traditional through the transitory popular to the avant garde. Had the first been less deep-rooted in England and the second less restrained and pleasantly acceptable, England's brilliant Edwardian furniture designers might have found greater confidence to forge ahead and might never have lost to Germany and Scandinavia their modern movement leadership.

Instead tradition commanded public respect: dignity and scrupulous workmanship graced the 'Elizabethan' or 'Jacobean' furniture for the dining room, the 'Louis' or 'Empire' for the drawing room and 'Sheraton' for the principal bedrooms. Ponderous dignity lingered through the period in clubs and grand hotels and the great liners associated with such decorators as Robert Whyte of Helensburgh. The grand pianos of Erard in London and Paris still displayed magnificent parquetry heavily adorned with hand-chiselled ormolu, but already collectors were being warned that the most splendid metal mounts could be reproduced cheaply as electrotypes.

J. A. Gotch in the *Art Journal* in 1904 suggested that nine-tenths of the furniture displayed in Tottenham Court Road and Oxford Street by such firms as Maple's, Hewetson, Waring, Gillow and Gill and Reigate was either copied from, or closely founded on, antiques. Well-made reproductions never lost their appeal, such as the £10 'Sheraton' cabinet illustrated in *The Queen* in 1913 by Mawer's Ltd who might show model and reproduction side by side. (By the 1920s John Barker and Company could offer a complete 'Cromwellian room' for under £50 or a 'Sheraton room' for under £100.) Even Liberty's in 1910 were offering 'facsimile reproductions of chairs and settees of the Stuart period'. Today these are valuable in their own right: in 1976 a wellington chest with marquetry in late eighteenth-century style stamped *Edwards and Roberts* (of Soho, London) was sold by Christie's of South Kensington for £420, a Maple's Edwardian Carlton House writing table for £300.

Popular architects—or their clients—tended to favour walls panelled below plasterwork friezes and ceilings often darkened with exposed beams. Murals might take the place of the Victorian's massed oil paintings, with the story theme continued, perhaps, in windows of coloured leaded glass and ceramics ranged along the panelling cornices. All this offered a somewhat cavernous setting for bulbous-legged refectory tables, high backed Jacobean chairs and stools and court cupboards on symmetrical twist-turned supports that now may pass as seventeenth-century work. Such firms as Hampton and Sons would include massive fire dogs flanking the grate, embossed candle sconces on the walls, perhaps a garnish of pewter in a recess above a low Jacobean dresser.

Sideboards were described as 'huge, heavy and bulbous' or 'refined and dainty in Sheraton style, gleaming with polish'. Ceramic plaques such as Wedgwood classical scenes were mounted on furniture again —even on metal bedsteads. Designs in the Gillow records of 1903–5 included bedroom furniture with panels of ornate carving, massive gadroons, fluted pillars with cup-and-cover swellings, suites worked out in laborious matching detail even to reel-turned towel rail. Typically, the important firm of Pratts of Bradford (one of the few firms to mark their products) in its 1901 trade catalogue declared that 'modern furniture designs consist very largely in the imitation of old styles' based on the seventeenth and eighteenth centuries. Use of modern machinery from the 1880s distinguishes their fine 'Hepplewhite' and 'Sheraton' chairs, but for a largely middle class public they dealt mainly in routine reproduction work such as florid carved detail on huge status-symbol hatstands.

Even here, however, the Olde English charade was only part of the story. For a time the firm were agents for trendy Liberty furnishings and in 1910 won a gold medal at the Brussels Fair for a desk of timeless simplicity, made attractive to traditionalists by its original name of the Duncan davenport.

Accepting then that the early 1900s were still deeply enmeshed in revivalism, the student can concentrate on furniture with a more original Edwardian flavour. The designer Walter Crane, President of the Arts and Crafts Exhibition Society, rejoiced that plain white or green paint had driven graining and marbling to the public house and by the 1900s there was considerable favour for light colour schemes and plain white walls. Lavinia Handley-Read has recalled that in 1911 when the architect Sir Edwin Lutyens restored Barham Court he insisted that all the paint work should be dead white, the panelling stripped to the natural wood, the cloth-less dining table set with plain white Wedgwood plates and green-handled knives. But even Lutyens complained that 'people don't know and don't care a dog's leg about architecture'.

Such settings welcomed furniture of the second main category which can be traced in exhibition work and commercial advertisement and forms the bulk of Edwardian furniture on the market today. But here again it is necessary to note its emergence out of late Victorian thought, when England led both in the social crusade of the arts and crafts movement and in *art nouveau*'s freedom of line and pattern.

The Edwardians' pleasure in newly established craft guilds prompted straightforward use of undisguised materials and construction techniques. At the same time, from 'that strange decorative disease', as Walter Crane called *art nouveau*, came a range of immediately recognizable and commercially exploitable ornament. The movement suggests a masculine ruggedness both attracted and repelled by *art nouveau*. The very men such as Mackmurdo and Voysey who first declared its language were appalled by the excesses of 'the squirm' in Continental furniture of the 1900s. Some, like C. R. Mackintosh, violently opposed it with emphatic patterns of functional straight lines and rectangles, yet were curiously involved with its elements of macabre fantasy. The period's most advanced designers never acknowledged it at all.

In the fashionable image of early Edwardian furniture, however, this combination of austere manhood and feminine wiles is important. Architect A. H. Mackmurdo had studied Italian Renaissance architecture and is credited (1886) with some of the first tall narrow shafts topped with wide flat caps that gave a welcome framework of contrasting angular emphasis to early Edwardian outlines on cabinet, bedstead and dressing table, for example, and suggested the silhouette for desk, chairback and wardrobe. These excessively long vertical members were widely popularized by the London architect of more than a hundred houses, C. F. A. Voysey, 1857–1941, whose plain oak furniture showed the metal designer's splendid handles and strap hinges. He designed for several firms such as J. S. Henry and Company and, like fellow designers Christopher Dresser and W. A. S. Benson, he saw the need to simplify, accepting machinery and ultimate cheap mass production.

Another leader sharing Voysey's ideals was M. H. Baillie Scott, 1865–1945, in Bedford from 1900 when J. P. White made his furniture. He shared, too, Voysey's many-sided interest in design and became well known for his later work at Letchworth Garden City and Hampstead Garden Suburb. His well-arranged built-in furniture combined the period's fashion for inglenooks with a foreshadowing of present day open planning. In furniture he might give a purely Edwardian flavour to cupboards painted white and decorated with daffodils and mottoes or design a timeless rushbottom chair.

Like Voysey he revelled in the copper, pewter and ivory ornament executed, for example, by the Guild and School of Handicraft. Indeed in many respects his work could be compared with that of the Guild's leader, the architect C. R. Ashbee.

Unfortunately Ashbee never reconciled idealism and costs. He was so troubled by the conditions he found when teaching in London's East End that in 1902 he moved his Guild group, some 150 men and their families, out to Chipping Campden where he 'sought to humanize work'. A small amount of furniture was made there to Ashbee's contemporary design, faulted perhaps by a tendency to cluttered ornament contributed by various guild craftsmen.

Ashbee appreciated the value of machinery and wished only to regulate the factory system so that men could do useful craft work 'without the haunting fear of workhouse for their families'. But a single heavy cabinet made in the Guild workshop might represent three months' labour for a craftsman at 50 shillings a week. As he noted in his book *Craftsmanship in Competitive Industry* even the country mood, 'this something that makes life good', was against them in the fight.

Lionel Lambourne has quoted a 1901 Vienna exhibition description of Ashbee furniture 'as if they came from a square planet inhabited by stout-built peasants, everything upright, angular at 90 degrees'. But he has stressed the importance of Ashbee's sense of mission and hatred of commercial standards, reflected most importantly by colleges of art throughout Great Britain under such leaders as W. R. Lethaby in London, Francis Newbery in Glasgow and E. R. Taylor in Birmingham.

It can be argued that Ashbee and his associates played an important part in guiding furniture design through its Edwardian transformation, away from squirming *art nouveau* ornament towards geometric austerity, while keeping largely to what was considered acceptable in the period's best trade work. Early Edwardian popular furniture, drawing widely on Voysey design, is recognized at a glance by those tall shafts topped with flat caps or rounded swellings, rising above bookcase and cabinet, bed head and dressing table mirror. In a chair back the side verticals may extend high above the crest rail and in a desk the whole outline may suggest a narrow T. The straight, square-cut legs are often so thin that they have to be introduced in groups or rows linked by low, wide stretchers or trestle feet.

Cabinet work tends to look flat in that it projects minimally from the wall. But there was great pleasure among designers in contrasts of hollow and projection at several levels so that on plan the front of a cabinet piece may show a series of angular zig-zags or alternating convex and concave curves, taken to extremes by such designers as J. S. Henry. Subsidiary but complementary is the early Edwardian upward-swooping curve, the shallow arch introduced over every sideboard recess and mirror glass, the cyma outlines to case furniture aprons and the 'jug handle' brackets flanking cabinets, desks and dressing tables.

These were the shapes advertised approvingly as quaint by Maple's, Oetzmann and other widely patronized furniture stores. Trade journals offered many designs, and the popular market was slow to abandon the style in multi-purpose furniture and the built-in seats and shelving of the cosy corner, derided as early as 1897 by R. M. Watson in *The Art of the House* for its 'ramshackle little shelves and peepholes' and premature decrepitude.

Shape in English work was seldom extreme but the student quickly observes the popular furniture market's interpretations of *art nouveau* ornament. Typically, those wide flower heads topping long stalks above rhythmic confusions of root were painted on chair backs, inlaid on cabinet panels, embossed in pewter and copper, worked in enamels and stained glass for cupboard and screen and exquisitely embroidered on soft furnishings. Like the ubiquitous hearts cut as apertures and shaped as strap hinge terminal, their assumed popular appeal persisted right to the end of the period, long after furniture had straightened out of its early Edwardian curves into bare coffer outlines. Even in such detail the period's gradual change of mood is revealing. Sinuous

[12]

stems soon yielded to groups of vertical lines, topped perhaps by plain ovals instead of endearing iris and sunflower, while ornamental turned spindles gave place to square-cut, vertical rails.

An early Edwardian cabinet by Morris and Company might be of fine Italian walnut, the glass-fronted cupboards enriched with curved moulding bars, their design repeated in the wavy lines of foliage in satinwood, sycamore and ebony. The successful firm launched by Morris and his friends in 1861 took over new premises and the current sophisticated ideas of the high quality furniture trade in the 1890s, and this is the furniture now found bearing Morris and Company labels. George Jack, 1855–1932, as chief furniture designer produced many a handsome glazed cabinet with swelling cupboards flanking a central complexity of pillared alcoves, the detail defined by the period's favourite checker outlines.

Other conventional designs were supplied to the firm by such architects as M. E. Macartney and by W. A. S. Benson, 1854–1924, of Hammersmith who was a director of the company. Benson's designs, like Jack's, were executed in the glowing woods of conservative fashion but with typical Benson emphasis on simple metal mounts. Even when the outlines were plain, Jack thought in terms of mahogany or walnut, ornamented in marquetry of sycamore, pearwood, satin-wood, holly, rosewood, cedar, ebony, at a time when more adventurous designers included mother-of-pearl, copper, pewter, stained glass. Hey-wood Sumner experimented with interesting incised work, gouging out hollows to be filled with coloured stoppings, introduced while hot and smoothed to the surface of the wood.

Even conservative Gillows might introduce copper grills on a 1903-5 wardrobe and 'leaded lights' in an asymmetrical design to harmonize with a washstand splashback of stencilled linoleum. Flat inlay and marquetry were the period's answer to the cheap ornament decried by *The Studio* with the comment, 'There are quite wonderful machines that turn out really hideous carvings'. (In 1902, for £11 10s, Norman and Stacey of Tottenham Court Road offered an 'artistic sideboard in fumed oak with oxidised copper grills and handles. Richly carved in bas relief, on panels and cupboard door, with twist turned corner pillars'.)

Early Edwardians still clung to the Victorian love of storytelling, and the shoulder-high lines of pattern across cabinet or bookcase might be replaced by carved words. The hall settle proclaimed WELCOME EVER SMILES, the wardrobe perhaps FINE FEATHERS MAKE FINE BIRDS. Such phrases suggested an outlet too for amateur talent: carving and poker work were popular hobbies then, with

Bookcase offered in oak, walnut or mahogany, entirely hand-made, with decorated panels in colours and brass or copper mounts, 3 ft wide. £7 9s, carriage paid. An advertisement by its designer, Henry T. Wyse of Arbroath, 1900.

leading stores offering tables, stools, bookcases, letter-racks, photograph frames, caskets, clock cases and so on for 'art painting', poker work or chip carving, some with period cabriole or ball-turned legs. Woods included oak, fumed oak and beech-stained oak as well as walnut, birch, sycamore and 'white wood'. Some were sold ready traced. But talented amateurs were often far more ambitious. The Rev. Leonard Staniforth, for example, carved a lychgate for his church, and his daughter Mrs Cardew remembers his care in choosing the blackberry spray to carve below the motto A PLACE FOR EVERYTHING AND EVERYTHING IN ITS PLACE stretched across the front of a massive, light oak desk. Here, as on an accompanying bookcase, every part of the surface is imaginatively carved.

High quality wood was important to Edwardians, and costly furniture may be of glossy satinwood, mahogany or walnut, with sycamore, holly and ebony introduced for contrasts of inlay or marquetry. Even at the cheap end of the trade many besides the aesthete agreed with *The Studio* in 1901 that to detest the french polisher was

[14]

the beginning of wisdom. 'Jacobean' dead black dye persisted to mask poor quality oak described by Frederick Litchfield, 1904, as covering all kinds of 'bad work, miserable construction, worse carving'. Still more cheap furniture was offered stained dull green or brown. Oak could be 'fumigated' to a fashionable dull tone with ammonia. Cheap rush-bottomed bedroom chairs were often of yellowish ash.

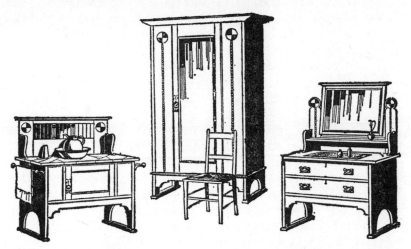

Bedroom suite including two chairs, of oak decorated with inlay, priced £8 17s 6d. An advertisement by The Midland Furnishing Co. in the Lady's Pictorial, *15 October 1910.*

To most of us the Morris firm is associated with charmingly simple furnishings for the English family's country cottage; and Edwardians may claim many other unpretentious chairs in light oak or ash with rush seats, often with the bold back verticals balanced by low stretchers. High Wycombe firms such as William Burch supplied Liberty's with interesting designs by E. G. Punnett, in the tall, severe manner.

W. S. Sparrow in *Hints on House Furnishings*, 1909, illustrates several plain, brown stained chairs made for Liberty's, with tall backs enclosing simple horizontal or vertical slats and with plain turned legs and thin double stretchers. These had the fashionable rush seats popularized in simple Morris chairs including the long proved 'Sussex'. Adorned with fancy-turned spindle backs and legs such simple designs might be offered as a 'quaint solid oak suite' fumed or stained green or brown, comprising settee, rocking chair, arm chair and four occasional chairs, priced by Oetzmann, for example, at £4 5s in 1903. Some of the simplest, most functional designs for light chairs are noted in the rounded, bent-wood work introduced by the Thonets of Austria and widely popular by the beginning of my period.

Harry Peach of Dryad, Leicester, issued many progressive cane designs meeting the cottagey needs of what *The Studio* in 1910 called 'our essentially open air race'. Such firms were the backbone of Edwardian furniture progress, including, for instance, J. S. Henry Ltd, Wylie and Lochhead of Glasgow and, most memorably, Heal and Son. At the time Henry's bold cabinet work was regarded as conspicuously progressive. Now his angular over-emphasis has a contrived and therefore dated look.

The same may be said of the influential Glasgow group known as The Four—Charles Rennie Mackintosh, 1868–1928, Herbert MacNair and the Macdonald sisters, fellow students studying applied arts, whom they married. Mackintosh is remembered for tall, starkly rectangular and triangular furniture, but the group's ornament, deeply influenced by Celtic imagery, included haunting female wraiths and swooping birds that earned them the name of the 'spook school'.

In Glasgow from 1885 Francis (Fra) Newbery was the Art School principal who encouraged Mackintosh, recognizing a strain of real originality. But Robert Macleod has noted that Mackintosh's influence was already fading by 1906: just for a brief spell he succeeded in combining 'British functionalism with a recognisable visual imagery'. Sir Nikolaus Pevsner suggests that in Mackintosh's design for the new Glasgow art school, 1898–9, not a single feature was derived from period styles: '. . . Building in his hands became abstract art, both musical and mathematical.'

For the furniture student an interesting detail here is Mackintosh's introduction of chiselling or wagon chamfering—just one of his many ways of using the wood surface's reflective gleam but one that later brought great praise to Gimson and the Cotswold furniture group. Mackintosh furniture designs in the Glasgow University collection include a white painted cabinet with slender formalized figure ornament inside the doors, in opaque, coloured glass against a silver toned ground. Cutlery that he designed in 1903 has a functional simplicity and grace that would look modern today.

The Glasgow architect George Walton, 1867–1933, was associated with Mackintosh for a time: Elizabeth Aslin credits him with converting the attenuated exaggeration of the Glasgow school into practical elegance. But by Edwardian days he was in London making conventional designs for Liberty's and other firms as well as for his own.

In London an architect and designer remembered for his influence on Edwardian furniture more than for his own restrained, substantial designs in unpolished oak was W. R. Lethaby, 1857–1931, who helped to found the Central School of Arts and Crafts. He joined with friends and pupils at the end of the nineteenth century to improve furniture standards with their own firm Kenton and Company. The venture lasted only two years, but of this group Ernest Gimson, 1864–1919, and the brothers Ernest and Sidney Barnsley had the private means to persist with their *avant garde* ideals. They established the Daneway Workshops at Sapperton in the Cotswolds in 1902, with Peter van der Waals, 1870–1937, from The Hague as foreman of cabinet making. Only the purist Sidney Barnsley, most clearly upholding their ideal that art was doing, not designing, carried out the actual manufacture of all his simple forthright oak furniture.

Gimson is praised today for a combination of simplicity and elegance in finely proportioned furniture mainly in English oak, elm, yew and walnut contrasted with inlays of ebony, rosewood and the like, every design created specifically for chosen materials. He never attempted, like Mackintosh, to escape from English tradition nor to influence or compete with the furniture trade, which he despised. Nevertheless his influence can be traced in all that has followed.

In the vanguard of Edwardian design, he may be regarded as the natural link between the arts and crafts movement and what Paul Reilly called 'the square spare bare period between wars'. In cabinet work large and small Gimson liked simple outlines, mainly low rectangles, their functional construction undisguised as might be expected of a son of an engineer, and the group was often condemned as losing a sense of style and dignity of design. Cabinets rested on simple strong-looking stands, their trestle legs perhaps linked at the back by trellis or vertical X-shaped stretchers, contributing to the flat look. Ornament might consist of extraordinarily fine close-knit marquetry in small formal patterns. Gimson—or was it Waals?—showed a fondness for chiselled edges to shelves, legs and other members. The light-catching wagon chamfering already noted on early Mackintosh work is pleasant when not tiresomely obtrusive. As might be expected, the metal work on Daneway furniture is superb.

An interesting detail noted in a Barnsley oak cabinet was the introduction of incurving scroll handles. Clearly use might cause these to mark the wood, so such potential damage was forestalled by cutting small crescent hollows where the rub would have come. Ornament on small Gimson cabinets and caskets may be very rich indeed with inlay of mother-of-pearl, silver, ivory, button bone and ebony or surface work in gesso or paint. A detail typical of its period is the painted decoration on some Gimson and Barnsley pieces by the potters Alfred

[17]

and Louise Powell who were closely associated with the Daneway group.

Designers so far described nearly all began with basic training in architecture, to serve clients of wealth and culture. But the other giant of the period was Sir Ambrose Heal, 1872–1959, trained from youth as an apprentice cabinet maker at Warwick. His reticent designs, beautifully proportioned, structurally sound, may be considered the first true foretaste of present day contemporary furniture.

When he joined his father's firm in 1893 it was from within the trade framework that he set out to transform furniture design for the well-informed, progressive-thinking middle classes. This is clearly stated in an interesting little catalogue issued by the firm in 1898, written by *The Studio*'s Gleeson White and illustrated with sketches by the architect C. H. B. Quennell.

This stressed that 'Messrs Heal make no pretence at any mission or desire to pose as pioneers in the cause of Art', but would be recognized as having done it stalwart service by all who were fighting for better things artistically. Demonstrating the theory that 'if a design is all right both constructionally as well as aesthetically, the workmanship is nearly always good also', Gleeson White drew attention to the firm's pioneer work with a metal dovetail. This resulted in a new popularity for wooden bedsteads made in walnut, oak or mahogany or, more cheaply, in ash stained green or brown.

Sir Ambrose showed a special facility in designing bedroom furniture. In his early work he shared, too, the arts and crafts enthusiasts' pleasures, such as pewter inlay. But his main concern was with unobtrusive good taste expressed in plain light-toned native woods, especially oak and sweet chestnut, suited to the fine proportions and gracious outlines of his style. To be noted, too, are many small constructional simplicities such as wooden turn-buckle fastenings, drawers cut with hollow hand-holes instead of metal handles, a flap perhaps where a drawer would be awkward below a wardrobe door. Nevertheless he could design, too, in grander mood, such as a bookcase, 1905, in magnificently grained Australian blackbean wood with inlay of mother-of-pearl in ebony bandings.

The basic movement seen in Edwardian furniture design can be traced even beyond the outbreak of war in 1914, as it settled into informed enjoyment of good design, unobtrusive construction and the sheer beauty of fine timber, leaving the colour excitement of pattern to printed and woven furnishings. As Lethaby had long foreseen, ornament had lost its relevance. It had been developed to protect and promote well-being but 'now that the magic has gone out of it . . . it will die . . . it will pass more and more out of the building custom of the future'.

Already in Edwardian days architecture and its associated crafts were becoming more and more impersonal. Germany by 1910 was thinking of furniture in terms of industrial design and in America modern unit furniture had taken shape. In England in 1915 talents developed in Edwardian days were drawn together in the Design and Industries Association. Led by Heal, Peach of the Dryad firm, the architect Brewer, the silversmith-potter Stabler, even veteran Lethaby, together with furniture craftsman H. Temple Smith, lithographer F. E. Jackson and printer J. H. Mason, this was a formidable stabilizing influence to meet the harsh bitterness of the 1920s.

3

Silver

EDWARDIAN silver is a wonderful source of tomorrow's antique treasure, still abundantly available but in mood already fascinatingly remote. In the 1900s traditionalists sought to prolong cloying, Victorian grandeur in an outburst of stylized glitter. But their competitors were a new generation of creative craftsmen, urgently excited by the sheer beauty of their material and eager to express their enthusiasm in the unacademic style of the thrusting natural world around them that they called *art nouveau*.

Significantly this short period produced work by more noteworthy silversmiths than can even be mentioned here. But sadly the heady excitement of 1900 soon faded. Against a commercial background of imitative historic styles the collector observes through early Edwardian days how the new silver's exuberance might be dispirited into acceptable quaintness, although elements of *art nouveau* persisted through the first three decades of the century. In church plate, of course, the architectural Gothic was still widely acceptable although generally lacking a scholarly approach, while Celtic and even Byzantine sources have been suggested to explain the Baroque extravagances of Omar Ramsden, for example, and Henry Wilson. But all too soon, even by the end of Edward's reign, silver shared in the general stiffening of design into angular unadornment, as recorded by the *Daily Telegraph*, 1910, when 'the beauty of art, even as the beauty of life, appears to be departing'.

By around 1900 the creative revival initiated by William Morris and his fellow Victorian rebels was at its peak, with arts and crafts ideals of sturdy, honest workmanship inextricably intermingled with the ornamental grace of *art nouveau*. C. R. Ashbee's Guild and School of Handicraft soon lost its driving force in the competitive battle for survival when it found rural peace at Chipping Campden from 1902. But by then this guild notion was everywhere taking effect: a romanticized interpretation of the medieval craft system sought to reunite designer and silversmith, sharing in honest traditional techniques. Even machine proud Sheffield had its Art Crafts Guild, with active silver designers and craftsmen, and Birmingham its Guild of Handicraft.

The enthusiasm expressed in all these new ventures was reflected in the training at such important centres as London's Royal College of Art (where Henry Wilson taught metalwork under W. R. Lethaby) and its Central School of Arts and Crafts. Birmingham had its Central School of Art and School for Jewellers and Silversmiths and there were many others. At its best the result was such an early Edwardian triumph as the Birmingham University mace by the firm of W. H. Haseler, Ltd, of Birmingham, 1902, every detail handmade and purposeful and rich in imaginative charm. Architect Philip Webb prepared its finely proportioned design and Robert Catterson-Smith, head of the Birmingham School for Jewellers and Silversmiths, supervised its workmanship. Both had been associated directly with William Morris, Webb as former chief designer for Morris and Company.

Towards the other end of my period the casket (Fig. 20) made in 1911 shows how Arthur Gaskin maintained the same ideals and the same admiration for exotic materials. He followed Catterson-Smith at the silversmiths' school and is remembered, too, with his wife Georgie for jewellery (Chapter 8). In this Jesse Collings Freedom Casket he used silver castings, *repoussé* and filigree work further enriched with gold berries, copper foliage, mother-of-pearl, niello work, blue beads of enamel and iron bosses damascened in gold.

This mace and casket show the period at its most magnificent. But collectors of Edwardian craftwork, handling even the simplest cup or spoon or candlestick, may trace a similar intense enjoyment in design and its translation, far from the contemporaneous commercial historicism and what Arthur Grimwade has described as a mass of effeminate, lacy piercings and stamped patterns trade-named as period styles.

Another leader in the craft tradition, Bernard Cuzner, looked back in his sixties and admitted the weakness of the craft movement, the challenges and opportunities missed by their refusal to come to terms with industry. Gilbert Marks, 1861–1905, for instance, at the turn of the century had his own workshop where he insisted on doing everything by hand. But C. R. Ashbee most clearly expressed the craft attitude to machines. He accepted them for rolling plate, for example, but not to shape hollow-ware by spinning. His mission was 'to determine the limits of the factory system', while questioning 'which are the things best made for their own sake, which best develop character and invention in the maker'. He saw machines disturbing the inventive power of his workshops and his anger was against the destruction of the craft revival 'by unregulated machine competition'.

Ashbee's own skill was as architect and designer, and his silver work was executed by the ten silversmiths involved with his Guild during its 21-year life: the mark *G of H L^D* was registered 1898. The Guild's eventual failure was partly due, he claimed, to the theft of his designs by London firms. His costing of a four-piece silver teaset in 1906, selling at £10, was not very different from London store prices. Today perhaps his daunting struggle is most interesting when viewed as the direct model for the Vienna workshops association of artist-craftsmen founded in 1903, although results were startlingly different.

How wonderfully flowing and individualistic Ashbee design could be, how sensitive to the grace of silver, is seen in the Painter-Stainers' Cup, 1900 (Fig. 15). Here the traditional, stemmed vessel follows the tall, upward-swelling outlines of its day but my attention has been drawn to the interesting fact that it is very similar to a silver-gilt steeple cup given to this ancient Livery Company in the seventeenth century, with London hallmarks for 1623.

The idea of ancient guilds was romanticized, of course, but these Edwardian dreamers experienced, as another of the period's architects, Charles Marriott, put it, the medieval craftsman's 'dumb conscience for the job, resembling the loyalty of the sailor to the sea, which comes not from artistic conviction but the sheer, and generally resented, discipline of tools and materials . . .'. The Artificers' Guild, for example, was founded in 1903 by Edward Spencer, remembered for much church plate, selling its wares in London, Cambridge and Oxford. Perth City Art Gallery has two shell cups on stone-set silver bases made by the Guild to designs by Spencer and J. P. Cooper. Another was the Bromsgrove Guild of Applied Arts, Worcestershire, with workshops and studios also in Birmingham, which by 1903 could boast of many international awards. Their range of crafts included gold and silver, ecclesiastical metalwork and jewellery, and they were associated with the important Birmingham firm of A. E. Jones.

The arts and crafts ideals that prompted such groups could be expressed particularly clearly in silver, based on a love of the material and trained mastery in its handling, that showed in affectionately hand-hammered surfaces, cleanly cut edges and delicate manipulation of wire and cable twists. These men took pleasure in openly declaring every constructional detail such as massive rivets. Inevitably weak imitations appeared—including even simulated rivets—but with so

1. Three-part screen, popular Edwardian setting for crowded figure scenes. This design by Kate M. Eadie catches something of prevailing medieval-romanticism; here the designs are worked on limewood, incised, stained and gilded. 1902. *Courtesy of the Victoria and Albert Museum.*

2. Sideboard in unpolished natural oak in the arcaded style of many arts-and-crafts furnishings around 1900, somewhat austere despite its flower and foliage inlay in ebony and sycamore. Designed by W. R. Lethaby, architect, author, influential founder-director of the Central School of Arts and Crafts, professor of design at the Royal College of Art and a Master of the Art Workers Guild. *Courtesy of the Victoria and Albert Museum.*

3. Dresser in elm wood designed by Ambrose Heal for the popular week-end cottage. When not in use, the wings fold over the central shelves to protect the dishes from dust. *Courtesy of Messrs Heal and Son Ltd.*

4. Small mahogany example of the Bradford desk, one of the most successful designs issued by the important furniture makers, Pratts of Bradford. This was advertised as 'accessible at all times yet instantly private at will' and won a gold medal at the Brussels Fair, 1910. The hinged flap opens forward and the roll-top is pushed back out of sight to reveal drawers, pigeon holes and inkwells. *Courtesy of Bradford City Art Gallery and Museums.*

5. Bookcase designed by Ambrose Heal, *c.* 1905, the frames and glazing bars of the cupboard doors suggesting the shape of an open book. This is in blackbean wood with bandings of ebony, inset with mother-of-pearl. The finely-figured Australian blackbean is difficult to cut in veneer but when well handled takes and retains a brilliant finish. *Courtesy of the Victoria and Albert Museum.*

6. Ashwood chair in country ladder-back style. This may have been made as well as designed by Ernest Gimson, before he launched the Daneway Workshops in 1902. Among the influences on his style was early study in an architect's office (J. D. Sedding) next to the Morris showrooms with their popular Sussex chairs, and this may have prompted his study of chairmaking under a Herefordshire pole-lathe chair bodger. The chair was used by his colleague Sidney Barnsley in his workshop. *Courtesy of Cheltenham Art Gallery and Museum.*

7. (*Right*) Cabinet and stand designed by Ernest Gimson. Typical of much Gimson work in its plain rectangular outlines, substantially based, its light-catching surface of small raised panels and rich ornamental detail. W. R. Lethaby noted of Gimson that every design was thought out for particularly selected wood: here, brown ebony is enriched with mother-of-pearl. The bright iron handles reflect Gimson's study of early English metalwork and the fine craftsmanship of Alfred Bucknell. *Courtesy of the Newarke Houses Museum, Leicester.*

8. (*Below*) Dresser of about 1905 recognizable as an Ambrose Heal design by its fine proportions and imaginative detail. The wood is light-toned sweet chestnut. *Courtesy of Messrs Heal and Son Ltd.*

9. Early Edwardian features in a Heal wardrobe, introduced in 1898. Here the wood is mahogany and the minor motifs in pewter inlay are given heart-shaped backgrounds in blue. Tall narrow door panelling and slightly arched panel headings balance the horizontal emphasis of the cornice, drawer section and pediment. An amusing detail, entirely of its time, is the motto FINE FEATHERS MAKE FINE BIRDS across the top in the period's high-shouldered lettering, ornamented with stylized peacock feather motifs. The bedroom suite includes a toilet table inscribed IF THIS BE VANITY WHO'D BE WISE? with the feather inlay flanking the looking glass. *Courtesy of Messrs Heal and Son Ltd.*

10. Dresser, 4 ft. 6 in. wide—Ambrose Heal's reply to the period's many ponderous sideboards. Here the customary high mirror is replaced by a single shelf in arch-crested lattice where the wood grain makes its own casual patterns. Typically this introduces no metal ornament, even the two cupboards being secured with a single wooden turnbuckle. In the rush-seated oak chair, too, the beauty of fine grain is the only ornament on wide rails and stretchers. This piece is interesting for its unobtrusive grace compared with Gimson's somewhat cramped early effort (fig. 6) and the tense, over-emphatic vertical lines of many a challenging Mackintosh chair, stained purple or green or painted glossy white. About 1906. *Courtesy of Messrs Heal and Son Ltd.*

11. Pierced 'George III' cake basket, a reminder that long-favoured traditional silver work was still welcomed by late Edwardians. The cast details in its asymmetrical scrolling borders include female masks among flowers, shells and butterflies. Made by D. & J. Wellby, 1910. *Courtesy of Sotheby's Belgravia.*

12. Hallmarked for the same year, 1910, as the cake basket above, this graceful vessel shows a little of what its designer C. R. Ashbee had been striving to achieve at his Guild of Handicraft. The circular body is shaped by hand hammering and the handle set with a chrysoprase. Length 7 in. *Courtesy of Sotheby's Belgravia.*

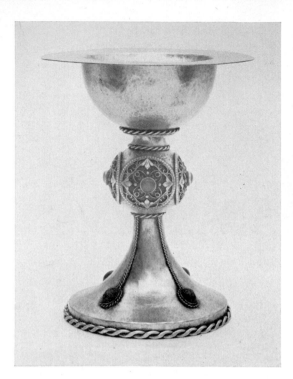

13. Demonstrating many arts-and-crafts features, this chalice and paten show perfect hand-hammered shaping in plain silver contrasted with extremely delicate piercing in the bosses applied to the spherical knop of the stem. Heavy ropework takes the rub of wear. Colour is introduced in red and deep blue stones roundly shaped in the manner of medieval jewels 'en cabochon'. By Sybil Dunlop, 1907. Height 7 in. *Courtesy of Sotheby's Belgravia.*

14. The up-thrusting plant growth of *art nouveau* lent itself especially to candlesticks, but here the applied stems and leaves have been controlled into satisfying stylized shapes below the wavy drip pans, while deliberately free of traditional form. These were designed by R. C. Silver as a youth for Liberty & Company and marketed as *The Conister*. They continued long in production: this pair bear the Birmingham hallmark for 1906–7. *Courtesy of the Victoria and Albert Museum.*

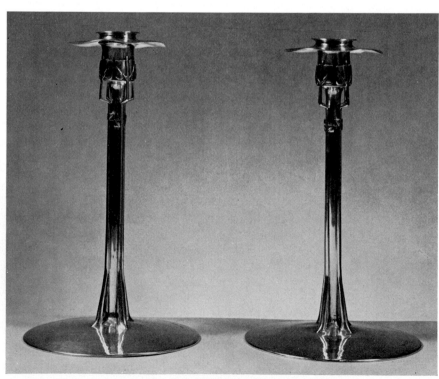

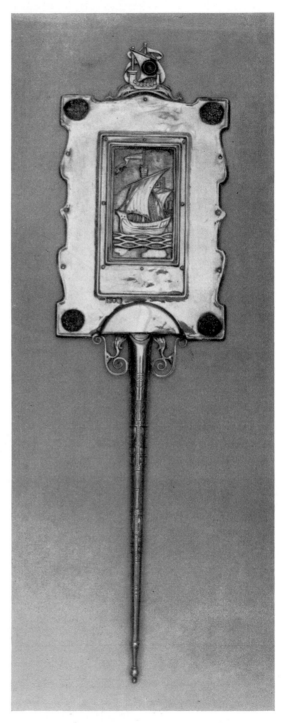

15 and 16. (*Above*) Traditional
design freely interpreted by C. R.
Ashbee in the magnificent Painter-
Stainers' Cup, 1900, essentially
dignified yet full of grace and
movement. Height 17¾ in. *Courtesy
of the Victoria and Albert Museum.*

(*Right*) Hand mirror, part of a set
by W. S. Hadaway, 1904, showing
another facet of the period's art
silver. The extraordinarily popular
galleon motif is embossed against
an enamelled ground of blue sky
and sea-green waves. Length 20½ in.
Courtesy of Sotheby's Belgravia.

17. Neat example of popular revived 18th-century ornament from a coffee and tea set made by the silversmiths Mappin & Webb in Sheffield in 1899. *Courtesy of Sotheby's Belgravia.*

18. In contrast, this art silver rosebowl shows a personal interpretation of Celtic detail by Bernard Cuzner, 1911. *Private collection. Photograph by courtesy of Birmingham City Museum and Art Gallery.*

19 and 20. Presentation caskets. (*Above*) With enamel plaques by
Alexander Fisher, about 1901. *Courtesy of Sotheby's Belgravia.* (*Below*)
The Jesse Collings casket by Arthur Gaskin enriched with gold,
copper, mother-of-pearl, enamel, niello and damascened iron, 1911.
Courtesy of Birmingham City Museum and Art Gallery.

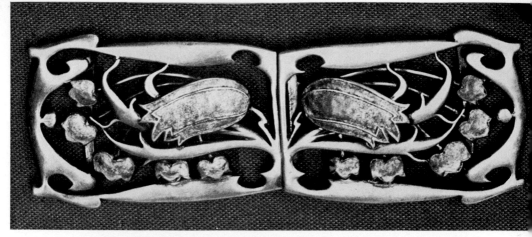

21. Dress buckles were never finer than in Edwardian days. The plainest were essential to secure the sportswoman's blouse and skirt but decorative art silver clasps might control the billowing Liberty silks of those in revolt against dress conventions. Liberty & Company sold many of these two-piece clasps, factory-made but cleverly suggesting costly hand craftsmanship. Here the repoussé silver framing is a foil for enamel work, the campanula flowers in mottled blue and mauve, the leaves green and yellow. This may have been designed by H. C. Craythorn and measures $4\frac{3}{4} \times 1\frac{3}{4}$ in. 1902. *Private collection. Photograph by courtesy of Birmingham City Museum and Art Gallery.*

22. Silver two-part clasp cast and chased to form the letters *ER* as a coronation souvenir. Made by Liberty & Company, who marked the occasion by issuing a number of coronation pieces such as silver spoons enamelled with crowns. Liberty designers generally remained anonymous unless their work was shown at arts and crafts exhibitions, but it is thought that this was designed by Archibald Knox. Its flowing curves are enriched with champlevé enamels in mottled blue, green and red. Size $3\frac{1}{2} \times 1\frac{1}{2}$ in. *Private collection. Photograph by courtesy of Birmingham City Museum and Art Gallery.*

23. Beaten copper rosebowl 7½ in. tall, of about 1900, by Leicester-born John Paul Cooper. The cover's pierced and engraved pattern of roses and leaves declares its purpose and a rose trellis forms the background to the dancing boys worked in repoussé around the stem. This attractive vessel shows but one facet of Cooper's skills which ranged from delicate gold wire and filigree jewellery to a revival in the use of shagreen. Cooper was exceptionally fortunate in his friends and associates. It was W. R. Lethaby who suggested he should study architecture under J. D. Sedding, giving him the stimulating companionship of Ernest Gimson and Ernest Barnsley. When he turned to metalwork in 1896 it was at the suggestion of another notable craftsman, Henry Wilson, with whom he worked before teaching metalwork at Birmingham and establishing his own workshop. (The Victoria and Albert Museum has a specimen showing his architectural approach to jewellery, a pendant containing a domed canopy over a Madonna and Child adorned with cabochon-cut jewels.) *Courtesy of Sotheby's Belgravia.*

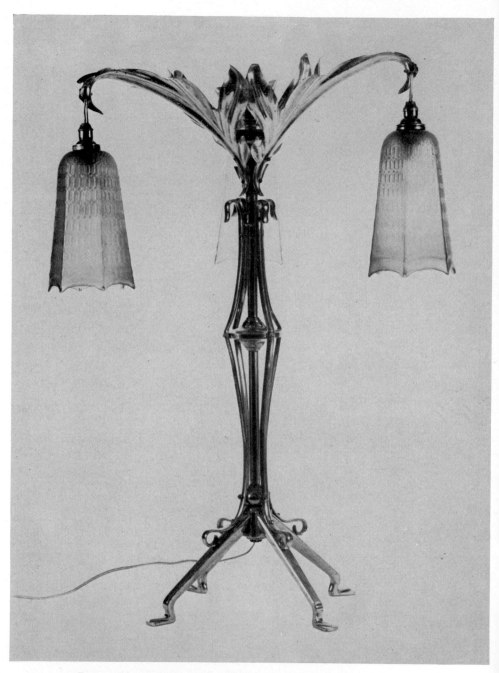

24. Brass and copper lamp by W. Benson & Company of about 1900.
The shapely acanthus leaves supporting the glass-shaded lamps are
of copper, as are the scrolls that give a cusped effect to the brass
column. Height 2 ft. 2 in. *Courtesy of Sotheby's Belgravia.*

25. Brass combined with glass in one of a pair of candelabra on brass-rimmed stands, made early this century: total height 6 ft. $1\frac{1}{2}$ in. The five branches are composed of brass-rimmed cut and moulded glass on a clear glass stem. The stand has a central baluster support with brass bands securing four free-standing glass pillars around it. *Courtesy of Sotheby's Belgravia.*

26. Hot water jug, cane handled, of about 1903, in Liberty's Tudric pewter, showing in crisp relief a simplified version of the swirling patterns applied to this firm's Cymric silver. As with much Cymric and Tudric ware, the jug's ornament shows obvious Celtic influences as might be expected of its probable designer, Manxman Archibald Knox, 1864–1933, who made over four hundred designs for the firm. *Courtesy of the Victoria and Albert Museum.*

27. Vase showing *art nouveau* influence in its flowing curves and petal rim. This is of copper with the three handles of brass. Height 6½ in. *Private collection.*

much fine work available these can be overlooked, as unimportant as the traditional patterns that still treated silver as neo-classic masonry or rococo shellwork.

The metal's mellow grey sheen was but one obvious reaction to the white glitter of electro-plate and the Victorians' artificial frosted and oxidized surfaces, just as its ornament with semi-precious coloured stones shaped *en cabochon* called scorn on sophisticated, faceted jewels. The intriguingly idiosyncratic John Paul Cooper, for example, revelled in all the appealing ornamental details then in vogue. He had met Ernest Gimson in his youth and shared his pleasure in extremely rich effects, using plain, heavy vessel shapes to display amethyst, chrysoprase, crystal, coral, ivory and lapis lazuli. He was importantly associated with the Birmingham Art School and with another major craftsman Henry Wilson, 1864–1934. Architect, sculptor, furniture designer (for Charles Trask and Company) and eventually Master of the Art Workers Guild, Wilson is given further consideration for his jewellery in Chapter 8.

Colour in association with silver at this time was especially effective in enamel work. This inexpensive jewel richness greatly appealed to the period's craft enthusiasts and was described in detail by the founder member of the Arts and Crafts Exhibition Society, Lewis F. Day. Sculptor-enamellist Alexander Fisher, for example, showed brilliant handling of its most exacting techniques in creative designs within unassertive silver framing. He accepted every challenge, revelling in colour intensities of this difficult but enduring medium and only regretting, among its users, a 'marked sterility of the imaginative faculty'. He admitted, however, that in difficult *plique-à-jour*, for example, one perfect result had to be set against about ten failures.

Around 1900 he was associated in London with Henry Wilson and Sir George Frampton, another sculptor who took up metal design and worked on important presentation pieces, all being involved with the Central School of Arts and Crafts. Fisher established his own Kensington School in 1904, his students including Nelson Dawson, whose wife Edith did most of the enamelling that enriched their delicately chased silver and jewellery (Chapter 8).

The popularity of swelling *repoussé* work may be more difficult to explain. Like many pseudo-antique home furnishings it harked back to the late seventeenth century and often contributed to the period's lingering pleasure in story-suggesting themes. There is some danger of triteness, of course, as in the hand mirror illustrated in Fig. 16, part of a dressing table set by W. S. Hadaway, but this designer-silversmith's work often shows great feeling for Celtic rhythms. Here

C

the galleon appears against an enamelled ground of blue sky and seagreen waves—an extraordinarily popular medieval-Edwardian motif, surely second only to the peacock, and found even on Liberty sets of silver buttons.

This sense of history was a strong feature of much of the period's costly plate. End-of-century excavations of Pompeiian silver renewed interest in Roman design, and wide use of Elkington electrotype reproductions had given the public a taste for classic grandeur. Exhibition silver had been especially the province of this great Birmingham firm but by Edwardian days they concentrated on domestic silverware. Only occasionally were their customers reminded of past glories and their most renowned designer Morel-Ladeuil, as when a rosebowl design of 1879 was reproduced in 1906, richly worked in high relief with classic figure scenes.

Research also produced much new factual information about early English silver, including hallmark identifications, prompting more careful copying. The London and Sheffield firm of Mappin and Webb included impressive tea wares chased with Renaissance ornament after Cellini and in the shapely rams'-heads-and-festoons neo-classic manner of Louis XVI.

By 1910 they were including silver copies of the late Georgians' adored Warwick vase but also fashionable, plain shapes 'hammered by hand'. But then this enterprising firm was prepared even to make a silver model of a tramcar for Sheffield Corporation in 1910, now part of the city's civic plate. Their repute is indicated by a commission from an Indian rajah in 1904 to make a silver bedroom suite. The firm's illustrated records show that this consisted of 16 pieces, including chairs, tables and a huge bed with life-size figures supporting a crowned dome and elaborate figure scenes in plaques on the head and foot boards. The total weight was almost one and a half tons.

Walter Crane recognized but regretted the lingering desire for something antique, encouraging 'the stimulation of past styles rather than original invention'. But he was equally apprehensive of *art nouveau*. This defiance of tradition was essentially youthful in its lyrical whiplash curves, its mystical faces among dreamy clouds of hair, its revolt against discipline, its vulnerability to despoliation in a hard commercial world. To many of today's collectors, growing up in the between-wars bleakness, those sensuous pencil-beguiling designs *were* art. Its excesses on the Continent soon brought satiety: even Van de Velde, first inspired as a designer by the sight of Liberty wares, later shared the current doctrine that the form of a vessel should spring purely from its function.

In England, it says much for Arthur Lazenby Liberty that when he took the lead in bringing *art nouveau* silver to the commercial market he left us so much that is immediately agreeable, although the work was produced in commercial quantities and so lacked the close designer-craftsman link that Ashbee demanded. In a period that saw something of a Celtic revival, it is not surprising to find a Celtic lilt to *art nouveau* design, in England as well as among the Glasgow Mackintosh school: this was acknowledged in the Liberty trade name of Cymric silver for the silver made for the firm from 1900 by the Birmingham factory of W. H. Haseler. Liberty's freelance designers remained anonymous but included, for example, Bernard Cuzner, A. E. Jones, Arthur Gaskin, Rex Silver and Jessie M. King.

A particularly sensitive designer for the Liberty firm in both silver and pewter was the Manxman, Archibald Knox. Yet even among outstanding Knox designs Shirley Bury notes in *Liberty's 1875–1975* that all but the most costly could be die struck. 'The Cymric school was always envisaged as a mass production exercise even while it incorporated the most recognizable features of arts and crafts work . . . Most of the hollow ware was either spun or die-stamped flat, complete with ornament, and then shaped.' Even hammer marks might be cut into the surface of the die. She suggests that Knox's control of line and a daring and highly original approach to the solution of functional problems 'smacks strongly of Dresser who habitually designed for machine production'.

A spoon with whiplash tendrils above the bowl was attributed by *The Studio* to painter-designer Oliver Baker, continuing some of the mannerisms of the brilliant sculptor and metal worker Sir Alfred Gilbert who left England for Bruges in 1909. Typically the bowl is in the heart shape then appearing alike in strap hinges and dining table menu holders and frequently as formalized foliage on whiplash stems.

Liberty designs received continuing admiration; the Cymric silver clocks in Egyptian pylon design have been noted with hallmarks for both 1900 and 1913. Only towards the end of the period was there a tendency for this work to lose its bold freedom and ornament to become niggling. Many other enterprising firms soon reflected the fashion, such as Asprey's, Elkington's, John Round and Sons, Edward Barnard and Sons and William Hutton and Sons.

Collectors with preconceived ideas about the new century's silver may be surprised to find how much of it allows the plain metal to be enjoyed, as in Ashbee's bowl (Fig. 12). Dresser's Victorian functionalism and personal interpretation of Japanese design were exceptional in their out-of-century severity but were captured successfully by Elkington's. Another Birmingham firm, Hukin and Heath, continued with some of his designs into Edwardian days. This firm had a liking for simple novelties, including, for instance, the familiar TOAST rack with the letters forming the divisions and the A enlarged as the handle. (The idea was developed for personalized gifts such as a pair for bride and groom forming their names.)

Other individuals deserve mention too, such as designer and metal worker Arthur Dixon, who followed the period's familiar pattern (not to be confused with the important Sheffield firm of James Dixon and Sons, for whom Dresser supplied designs). He studied architecture, becoming a friend of Morris and an important figure in the prolific Birmingham Guild of Handicraft. His interest in a wide field of metal crafts was shared by another important architect and designer, W. A. S. Benson, whom I have mentioned earlier as a director of Morris and Company. Benson was exceptional in the extent to which he was prepared to flout arts and crafts theories and accept the cost-cutting benefits of machinery, even of spinning and stamping. His own Hammersmith factory supported a Bond Street shop and supplied Bing's Paris shop L'Art Nouveau.

The tax on silver had been removed in 1890 and this period expected silver for innumerable minor items, interesting to collectors today for their associations. Georgian Sheffield plate and still cheaper Victorian electro-plate had accustomed middle class homes to a vast array of glittering sideboard dishes, teawares, centrepieces. Any wedding gift list will confirm this. Probably over half the gifts would be in this status-symbol material (appropriately crest engraved, if possible) from card cases and sovereign purses to the perpetual

From an advertisement by the Goldsmiths and Silversmiths Co. in The Connoisseur, *June 1908.*

calendars known as date stands and small casters for spicing tea-time muffins, then known as muffineers.

It is very certain that Edwardians enjoyed their silver, even to the trite mottoes on visiting-card trays for the hall and the embossed cherubs that persisted from Victorian days on table centres, candelabra and cake baskets, only losing ground late in my period to somewhat petty, flat chasing and catchy Greek key piercing. Even a little of the whimsy found in costume jewellery enlivened minor work, which by then included much silver equipment for card games, dominoes and draughts as well as smokers' cigarette boxes, match cases, cigar cutters and other accessories mentioned in Chapter 9. Towards the end of the period there was a marked interest, too, in children's silver with nursery rhyme characters on 'pusher and spoon' sets and fairies around the toilet mirror as an alternative to Reynolds' *Heads of Angels*.

Silver miniatures for adults were never better, such as a tiny, silver-mounted, wooden tray loaded with a champagne set or miniature smoking equipment, or a twelve-piece tea and coffee service complete to the last teaspoon. In normal sizes, spoons were remarkably varied, from crested souvenirs in the fashion shared with Edwardian Goss china to all manner of newly popular novelties to go in the tea caddy.

Photograph and mirror frames abounded, most easily recognized today when ornamented in *art nouveau* asymmetry with coiling leaves and long sinuous stems and the occasional female with flowing hair. For the dressing table a pair of candlesticks and matching easel mirror was still a popular choice as was the ubiquitous ring stand, sometimes representing a tree, occasionally a deer's antlered head (now yet another collector's by-way). Innumerable cases of silver were offered by the department stores, with hollows suitably lined in blue silk or velvet to hold bonbon dishes, condiment sets, fish servers and the like. In many, however, the silver was disastrously thin to facilitate the press stamping that was in itself conducive to sameness in design even when it included debased *art nouveau* detail.

It is rare in English work to find the extremes that excited the Continent in either the whiplash flourishes of *art nouveau* or the austere geometry of Vienna's Josef Hoffmann, but the latter, too, might be echoed in an occasional piece, for example, by the Sheffield firm of John Round and Sons. At the other extreme was Omar Ramsden, 1873–1939, Sheffield born and trained although he appears to have sought little subsequent association with the city. With his partner Alwyn Carr he is remembered for a style of mannered medievalism in ornate church and ceremonial plate that sets them somewhat apart from their fellow silversmiths. They favoured Holbeinesque design, giving a certain unnatural grandeur to quite minor pieces. This was part of the mystique Ramsden acquired even in his own working lifetime, typified by the style of slightly pompous inscriptions usually found on even the simplest salt cellar: *Omar Ramsden et Alwyn Carr me fecerunt*.

Ramsden was widely travelled and a frequent lecturer. The value of his personal contribution to his St Dunstan's workshops as either designer or business manager has been questioned, but at least these workshops produced craftsmen who were highly proficient in chasing and engraving and associated skills, successfully turning out piece after piece of cathedral and university plate. And when in about 1908 the renowned designer Lewis Day wanted a napkin ring made for his wife it was to Ramsden and Carr that he entrusted the work. The year 1914 marked the end of their partnership. But in 1913 a future apprentice in the Ramsden workshops had been born, Leslie Durbin.

*   *   *

Electro-plated silver became established half a century before my period but continued to follow in the wake of Edwardian silver design. Elkington and Company were still reminding customers that they were 'the originators of electro-plating' on a souvenir match holder they made for the 1901 Glasgow Exhibition. Endless copying of eighteenth-century silver inevitably produced many terrible hybrids.

Tea and coffee service in 'Chippendale' design advertised by Mappin and Webb Ltd. Priced as shown at £36 1s in Princes plate; £80 5s in silver (of which the tray cost £44). Advertised in The Connoisseur, *December 1907.*

But *art nouveau* ornament appeared too, some given a grey patina to suggest craft silver and tone down the white brilliance of the unalloyed silver thinly covering this electro-deposit plated ware.

Among customary tablewares the main problem remained the thinness of the silver plating and frequent need of re-silvering, widely advertised even in the 1930s. Hence the popularity of wear-masking, all-over flat chasing, on such items as a plated tea tray that might most quickly be polished down to the yellowish grey of the underlying nickel alloy. Here an exception was the Mappin and Webb Princes plate marked 'Triple Deposit' and 'guaranteed to wear like sterling silver for 30 years'.

The Elkington firm improved manufacture of their spoons and forks, shaping them from the flat, and often tipping the forks with solid silver. But many of us must remember the disappointment of pearl-handled fruit knives and forks, for example, with ferrules of hallmarked silver but proving by smell and taste to have worn-away plating in blade and tines, to ruin the flavour of the fruit: the shrewd Edwardian still carried his own folding gold or silver fruit knife, often combined with a nut pick.

A continuing pleasure in novelties gave the Edwardian such curiosities as the combined fruit knife and orange peeler and all manner of matching sets such as the three-piece 'universal servers'—spoon, fork and slice—and the four-piece set for coping with lump and caster sugar, butter and jam. Small tongs for eating asparagus were sold in boxed sets, as well as the large asparagus servers and other spring-fitted tools for catching elusive pickles.

A small dish, gilt inside, with a tall leafy handle was designed to suspend a bunch of grapes (served, of course, with ornate grape scissors). Various trefoil breakfast dishes were devised, fitted for toast, egg, condiments, butter or marmalade, and there were plated, shell-shaped, spoon warmers for a generation that still expected gilding on the bowls of the plainest egg spoons and ornament all over their fish knife blades, from ivy leaves to willow pattern.

An adaptation of the electro-deposit process produced the period's interesting electrotypes or galvanos. Rare original models were exactly mould-copied in wax or other easily melted composition, brushed with blacklead to make it conductive so as to receive an electro-deposit of copper. The wax was then melted and the same electro-deposit process coated the inside of the copper shell with a layer of silver. Muriatic acid dissolved the copper, but a collector may find a tell-tale granulated surface on the silver's underside, for example inside an ornate tea caddy.

[29]

4

Copper, Brass and Pewter

IN days of ever flimsier electro-plated glitter, solid base metals were at the very heart of the arts and crafts movement. Fine trays and bowls were hand hammered from copper and brass sheet and chased and pierced with patterns of briar rose or interlaced hearts, while candlesticks stylized the thrusting lines of plant growth.

Much metal work stemmed from architects' concern to find appropriate house furnishings. Typically, the popular architect C. F. A. Voysey was described in 1909 as designer of 'everything necessary for the equipment and decoration of a house', down to faceted iron pokers and tongs. Edwardian remodelling of Debenham and Freebody's shop required designs for all the bronze, brass and iron work, the electric fittings and wrought iron balconies, from C. A. L. Roberts of Birmingham. Several leading designer-teachers were thus lured away from architecture, such as Henry Wilson and J. P. Cooper. I mention these craftsmen when considering jewellery: other jewellery-silversmiths interested in brass and copper included Harold Stabler and Bernard Cuzner. When designing for the London Artificers Guild, Edward Spencer might combine silver with wrought iron, copper and bronze. His domestic work included bowls and candlesticks and the inkpots that were still important at this time and are now collectable minor items, in silver and base metals in a score of fancy shapes including patented portable designs.

Some important arts and crafts leaders revelled in simple brass and copper vessels, such as Llewellyn Rathbone of Liverpool and London, who executed some of Voysey's designs, and Arthur Dixon of the Birmingham Guild of Handicraft. Ernest Gimson, of the Daneway Workshops, had a great feeling, too, for magnificent polished steel as had the brilliant blacksmith Alfred Bucknell who carried out his projects. Leicester Museum has some polished steel firedogs and a fine brass Gimson-Bucknell pitcher, and Cheltenham has copper candlesticks and sconces.

In Glasgow not only The Four (see Chapter 2) but many other

craftsmen such as Talwin Morris, George Walton and Marianne Wilson contributed interesting work in beaten copper and polished iron. MacNair's wife, Frances Macdonald, taught metalwork at the School of Art from 1907, and Glasgow Museum has some of her beaten brass and tin. Her sister Margaret has left a number of tall rectangular metal panels containing typical formalized female figures.

I have mentioned already the simple practical designs by W. A. S. Benson, welcoming machine techniques to replace much time-honoured noisy bench work. But Christopher Dresser, still active right to his death in 1904, was the period's most forthright exponent of machine-determined functionalism. His sparse designs required minimal quantities of common metal sheet from the rolling mill, finished merely by lathe polishing.

Numerous groups of London and provincial craftsmen held annual exhibitions such as the Home Arts and Industries Association, the Haslemere Peasant Industries and the Working Ladies Guild. A few names of individuals are remembered, too, such as Herbert Maryon of Reading, Florence Rimmington, George Rushton of Ipswich, Robert Emerson, J. A. Hodel of Liverpool, Frank Clarkson, S. M. Martineau, Ernestine Mills, Walter West. But only occasional Edwardian marks are found, such as *KSIA* used by the Keswick School of Industrial Art on hammered brass and copper. Artist-designer-silversmith Harold Stabler was a director here before joining Llewellyn Rathbone to teach metalwork at Liverpool; both subsequently taught in London. Initials *JP* on a hammered copper basket or salver may be those of John Pearson, one-time metal instructor for Ashbee's Guild of Handicraft.

Today collectors look for trays, bowls, photograph and mirror frames in *repoussé* copper and brass, inset perhaps with roundels of Ruskin pottery (known as Ruskin stone) or coloured enamels. Copper plaques were made for setting into furniture and bronze castings for wall ornament. Even motor car mascots from the period are now collected, including the most famous Rolls Royce, *Spirit of Ecstasy*, designed by Charles Sykes in 1911.

Candlesticks offered opportunities for sturdy arts and crafts hammer-work as well as wild *art nouveau* ornament: H. U. Haedeke saw this as the last manifestation of the candlestick as an individual article with function subordinated to aesthetic appeal, its stem swaying in the breeze and drifting leaves and blossoms to contain the socket.

The Edwardian metal craftsman's Bible was Henry Wilson's *Silverwork and Jewellery*. Here is much sensible criticism of current practice such as 'the modern vice of putting in hammer marks to make a bad form look well', and technical advice on such matters as colouring bronze alloys. But less arduous instructions were available too, such as the Gawthorps' *Art of Brass Repoussé*, 1907, offering instructions for making 'ornaments and knick-knacks' for sales and bazaars. 'Very large numbers of ladies in America and England have taken up this work and are diligently hammering away . . . '.

They recognised that it had become difficult for the amateur to compete since 'much that was a few years ago hand wrought is now struck from costly dies or electrotypes (under fancy names) from models, for instance, panels for furniture, sconces, brush backs, jardinières, door plates, etc.'. Nevertheless they saw prospects for well designed, carefully worked menu holders, finger plates and the like in brass or pewter, perhaps, or in copper chemically bronzed, a process which was 'difficult and unpleasant'. Gawthorp and Sons of East Finchley could supply all tools and materials—and for leather work and bent iron work too—and offered as a final inducement 'amateur work made up and polished inexpensively'.

Already, however, Edwardian brass and copper, along with black-varnished fancy iron work, was dominated by commercial products, whether from Birmingham or Benares, as lamented by C. R. Ashbee who saw the hammerman and chaser (coppersmith) driven out of business by the department stores' abundance of imitation *repoussé* stamped by machine. Liberty's still imported largely from Cairo and Damascus, such as brass trays and coffee pots inlaid with silver and copper, but by then the 'Arab' vogue was yielding to the beaten brass and copper panels ornamenting furniture in *art nouveau*. H. U. Haedeke noted how increasingly skilful mass methods could ruin the spirit of *art nouveau*, producing shining brass desk equipment and the like with the characteristic motifs but conveying 'no feeling for quality nor for the inherent properties of the material'.

Even these, as recorded in Edwardian stores' catalogues, now have a certain nostalgic appeal, the brass often showing hammermarks and sometimes offered as 'antique' with a 'tarnished finish' preserved by clear lacquer; the copper often oxidized. The items most popularly enriched with those 'characteristic motifs' ranged from curbs with matching fire-dogs for the 'brasses' to crumb trays and their sickle-shaped brushes. Fire screens were popular in *repoussé* brass and copper and with panels of leaded stained glass or painted mirror glass, and for coal there were buckets, helmets and boxes of all shapes.

Many items, however, have a purpose-made usefulness about them that makes exact dating difficult, such as innumerable Edwardian oil lamps (even Longleat used oil until 1930) and candlesticks in saucer shapes. The perforated brass cylinder style should include a glass shade and long-stemmed extinguisher. Brass door porters continued the dome base and long hook handle; tin-lined copper moulds for entrées and desserts followed traditional shapes such as crescent moons, smiling suns and piles of fruit, although machine-stamped in lightweight metal. Only the war dimmed the popularity of jardinières on their scrolling stands and copper kettles on similar writhings of wrought iron. The Army and Navy Stores' 1907 catalogue offered its members a brass and copper 'gipsy kettle' with rustic handle hooked on a rustic arch above the spirit lamp.

The list is endless, from Westminster chime dinner bells to bedroom hot-water jugs ridiculously textured to suggest crocodile skin (which the careful maid covered with one's towel, making it warm but soggy if one slept late). Already deliberate reproductions were on the market such as long-outmoded brass pipe stoppers, door knockers (from the Durham Sanctuary lion's head to the Lincoln Imp) and chimney figures such as characters from Dickens.

Today a few collectors look for Edwardian horse brasses such as easily dated souvenirs and portraits and the popular mementoes of those magnificent railway horses that filled the cobbled yards with clattering jingle. Many were stamped from soft-textured spelter brass but the collector must come to know the look and feel of old and long-rubbed brasses while picking cautiously among the many modern, poor-surfaced castings.

Other collectors look for the nostalgic Edwardian gimmickry of biscuit tins which then could be directly printed in full colour to masquerade as a pile of books, perhaps, or a miniature gipsy caravan. This sales appeal was at its peak throughout my period and has left innumerable boxes shaped and printed as tin motor cars, handbags and the like along with such curiosities as old master paintings reproduced on canisters that could stay in use as string holders. (To me *The Boyhood of Raleigh* will always be associated with kite-flying.)

To many a collector, however, the Edwardians' most intriguing base metal was pewter. This amenable alloy may be found in bluff arts and crafts shapes and patterned with what John Houston has called the 'ecstatic stress and strain' of *art nouveau*, in bowls, lamps, candlesticks and furniture plaques, even in commercial wares from church plate to menu holders and in commercially encouraged amateur concoctions—a summary that still oversimplifies the story.

Definitions are important here. Makers and collectors alike at this time were at pains to differentiate between pewter and britannia metal. Only within the last few decades has britannia metal come to be accepted as closely related to the early pewterers' finest leadless ware. From a collector's viewpoint the practical difference lies in the alloys used to strengthen the ancient metal men's precious tin: copper to make bronze for casting; copper and bismuth in high quality pewter, with lead for cheaper variants; antimony with a trace of copper probably in some early 'leadless pewter' and in my period's invaluable, widely-made britannia metal.

All these alloys can be cast into splendid tablewares and the pewterers' traditional crafts were continued when castings were hammered into compact strength and finished with lathe-turning to leave no visible trace where cast sections were joined by highly skilled soldering. But sonorous britannia metal became important because it allowed lighter and more decorative treatments (flimsy according to its detractors). As a thin metal sheet it could be cut, drop-stamped and soldered. And it could be raised into hollow ware, not by hammering, but by holding it against a wooden or steel chuck spinning in a lathe. The final achievement was machine polishing to a bright silvery tone tinged with blue and lacking only silver's sparkle.

As britannia metal spread from the Vickers factory, Britannia Place, Sheffield, to many other factories, it acquired such a reputation through the nineteenth century as a cheap, lead-free alloy that Edwardians accepted it for innumerable workaday wares, from teapots and biscuit boxes to ashtrays and inkstands. Today these are no longer silver-bright but still have a mellow gleam unless pitted through long neglect. Another Sheffield firm, James Dixon and Sons, became outstanding among the city's seventy-odd early nineteenth-century makers.

The silversmith's shapes might be followed, soldered from parts made by machine-stamping and loaded with cast feet, spouts, finials and fancy ornament. The metal even suffered the indignity of being used as a base for electro-plating with pure silver so thin that often it has been polished right away, its short-lived white glitter recorded by the letters E P B M (electro plated britannia metal) stamped on the base, where tyro collectors may try to translate pattern numbers as a date.

The main clue for Edwardian dating appears on tavern measures and then it indicates only the vessel's capacity testing or retesting by the Board of Trade. From 1878 this was recorded in a standardised mark consisting of monarch's cypher (ER and GR for my period) and a number representing the county or borough of the testing officer—522 for London County, 19 for Derby County, 64 for Sunderland and so on.

Time was when traditional pewter manufacturers claimed their pollutant-free metal supreme for ale tankards and measures, vinegar funnels and ice-cream moulds. But too many Edwardians thought of the ware in terms of heavily leaded, ley metal (the lead becoming limited by law to ten per cent as late as 1907 in the poorest quality pewter). At that lead-conscious period, when even pottery buttons might advertise their lead-free glaze, everyone had a horrific tale of pewter coffee spoons that were visibly diminished by stirring the hot liquid. There was, too, the Edwardian drinker's wish to see the colour of his lighter ales, not fully met even in glass-bottomed tankards. And hostesses found that table desserts could be turned out as far more elaborate undercut ornaments when the cook used clever two-part or three-part moulds die-stamped from britannia metal.

Then, when cast pewter was almost ousted from taproom and kitchen, the Edwardians saw a fascinating revival of it, attributed by the authority H. H. Cotterell to 'its inherent artistic loveliness'. In 1885 London's one remaining firm of high quality manufacturing pewterers, Brown and Englefield, entered a float of medieval pewterers in the Lord Mayor's show, scattering souvenir medals among the crowds. Praise for the 'venerable craft' from Starkie Gardner and others was followed by books for collectors by such enthusiasts as H. J. L. Massé in the early 1900s; exhibitions were organized in London and Scotland and a collectors' society was founded in 1918 that now includes britannia metal under the modern term lead-free pewter. All this despite warnings in *The Connoisseur* in 1901 by L. Ingleby Wood that already pewter was being cast from old moulds 'in very base metal indeed' on the Continent for British and American tourists.

Among Edwardians this admiration for antique specimens led to the discovery of pewter as a marvellous medium for arts and crafts enthusiasts. Just how splendid it could be is illustrated by Elsie Englefield in her *Short History of Pewter* with a 26½ inch high candelabrum made by her father W. J. Englefield which he presented to the Pewterers' Company when he was Master in 1910. This was designed by Harold Stabler, and Cotterell noted that the bowl shapes supporting the candle arms were hammered from flat sheet metal, pierced with lettering and linked by a stem bearing the Company's arms in relief while the cast finial was the Company's patron saint, the Virgin Mary.

Germany especially pioneered this pewter rediscovery, and A. L. Liberty obtained supplies from Nuremberg, Krefeld and Munich until comparable English work was available, supplied by Haseler of Birmingham, a self-confessed collector and fanatic about pewter. Addressing the Royal Society of Arts in 1904 on *Pewter and the Revival of its Use*, Liberty noted that the modern artistic ware contained no lead ('except Japanese in their antimony ware'), being composed of tin alloyed in the proportion of five per cent of 'antimony or bismuth or both'. This was a much smaller proportion of antimony than in the brittle, modern, German pewter that permitted sharp relief castings but resulted 'when bent or bitten' in the well-known crackle or *cri*.

Liberty saw pewter as 'essentially a homely metal'. The motifs and lines of ancient Celtic ornament, applied with such success to his firm's Cymric silver, could be applied to pewter too, he decided, but only in modified form, emphatically with no attempt to imitate the precious metal and soon supplemented by plant motifs. This Tudric pewter was developed 'under the fostering care' of his colleague John Llewellyn, a director of the Liberty-Haseler company, Liberty & Co. (Cymric) Ltd.

Liberty's Tudric pewter was in production by 1902 and is now eagerly collected—squat little tea and coffee services, tall upswept candlesticks, flower bowls, cake stands, plaques, clock cases, cigarette boxes. Their soft grey surfaces were frequently hammer marked, sometimes touched with enamels and patterned in relief or stencil-cut in graceful, stylized plant motifs such as honesty and cyclamen. Some Liberty favourites continued in production until the Second World War, and through my period lush *art nouveau* designs were produced by other firms too, such as Hutton and Company of Sheffield and Connell of Cheapside, London. In 1907 the Army and Navy Stores devoted two full catalogue pages to 'the new art pewter ware' including trays, candlesticks, table dishes and glass-lined bowls and biscuit boxes.

The Englefield firm continued, too, with their traditional methods of casting sturdy pewter vessels—tankards, jugs, sugar casters and the like—from the gun metal moulds acquired by the firm over the past two hundred years. Confectioners' goods, measures and so on were burnished bright, but candlesticks and flower bowls were treated to preserve the pewter's natural soft tone.

For Edwardians the last phase in the pewter story was its establishment among the crafts offered in neat outfits to amateurs, along with the whitewood articles for chip carving and the hammers and punches for amateur *repoussé* ornament in copper and brass.

In a manual in the Artistic Practical Handicraft series F. J. Glass, head of Doncaster School of Arts and Crafts, offered full instructions, from the simplest button or hatpin head to hollow-ware shaped from thicker gauge metal by raising and annealing. Soldering was difficult with such soft metal but the veriest beginner could achieve results in amenable pewter with smooth-faced steel modelling tools and a few punches to fill the backgrounds. In 1913 Gamages offered all the familiar art motifs—peacocks and poppy heads, lizards, irises and the like—on items from serviette ring to pencil box. They had a lady demonstrator to prove how easy it all was, and offered patina pewter colouring at 7½d a bottle.

*   *   *

Buttons in *art nouveau repoussé* patterns are to be found in silver and pewter but by Edwardian days far more were stamped in brass and gilt metal. They offer endless opportunities to collectors, for many can be identified, made for the armed services, civilian officials, huntsmen, liveried servants. England had a reputation for strong brass buttons but at this period materials ranged from cameos to carved and painted crystals (Chapter 8). Here again the period's favourite colours are to be found—greens and blues and tawny reds—in the glossy earthenwares of the Ruskin and Lancastrian potteries. Many buttons are marked—silver hallmarks on the front or a maker's mark, such as Firmin, around the shank.

Haberdashers still stocked multiples of six or five and these, boxed or fixed to cards, are a special delight to the collector, with no memory of cold mornings when a score or more of the small tyrants might bar a child's way between icy bedroom and hot breakfast. As Gwen Raverat commented in *Period Piece*, there must have been something aristo-cratic about buttons in those days for everything that could possibly button and unbutton was made to do so—nightgowns, sleeves, bodices, drawers. My own especial childhood misery was a pair of inherited leather gaiters buttoned tightly all down my protesting legs with a hostile buttonhook, from a silver-handled set of hook, shoe horn and glove stretcher.

In pre-zip days hidden hooks and eyes could achieve the essential smooth fit to each layer of costume but buttons could do this graciously, with individual charm. Sonia Keppel in *Edwardian Daughter* recalls a spring dress of her mother's, striped grey and white. Below a boned high collar it cascaded in widening folds to the waist 'and from her throat to her knees it was buttoned with tiny braid buttons'.

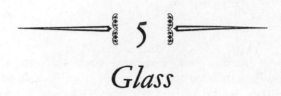

Glass

'THE last fifty years have witnessed greater changes in the glass industry than any other,' declared Harry J. Powell in his book *Glass Making in England*, written shortly before he died in 1922. 'The conception of the material itself has changed ... Varieties of glass ... are now numbered by the hundred ...'

Edwardian artist-glassmen shared with artist-potters in the aesthetic pleasure that came with the period's technical advances, based mainly on exact heat control and colour chemistry. Many improved the skills demanded by current fashion: a few such as Powell himself showed a new sensitivity to their marvellous medium, promoting wider acceptance of fluid forms, expressive textures and new subtleties of colour. For the rest, there were such marvels as the plate-glass mirror over 200 feet square cast in front of the king and queen, the hand-carved neo-classic cameos and the miraculously cheap and colourful 'toys' now so eagerly collected.

Edwardians perhaps took it all too much for granted. For over two centuries British flint-glass (now called lead crystal) had been world renowned. Now British glassmen had mastered the techniques—and won the exhibition medals—for decorating it to every man's fancy. Their achievements included cutting and engraving (frosted or shiny-polished, in cameo and intaglio) and colourwork that could make it gleam like old ivory, glitter like aventurine and dazzle with iridescence.

At this time the industry was largely centred in the Stourbridge area of the west Midlands, but there were also Powell's important London Whitefriars Glasshouse, still in the shadow of St Paul's, much interesting activity in Scotland and thriving pressed glass works around Gateshead and Newcastle.

The intense refractive fire of British flint-glass had always favoured deep-cut ornament and this had been in and out of fashion throughout the nineteenth century. At the beginning of my period cut glass astonished its admirers with its mathematical precision and technical sophistication. But by then those who loved its sparkle were opposed by a growing body of purists supporting Ruskin's condemnation of such 'barbarity'. Instead, as in all branches of the arts and crafts movement, there was a new concern for form in relation to this fluid metal. Even fashionable Harrods in 1895 acknowledged 'the growing demand for Plain Table Glass' in tall slender shapes.

For the more conservative customer, however, intricate geometrical cutting still added ever-increasing brilliance to the period's vast suites of decanters and glasses, then customarily numbering 85–86 and sometimes over 200 for home and prospering export sale. R. Wilkinson in *The Hallmarks of Antique Glass* illustrates items from an early twentieth-century 216-piece suite, one of each dozen signed by the Stourbridge engraver J. Lloyd. According to Wilkinson, one Stourbridge factory even allowed pensioner-cutters their own workshops to elaborate unhurriedly on the skill they loved. And the most highly skilled craftsman, the lapidary cutter, made innumerable finger-pleasing stoppers for decanters, spirit bottles and perfume flasks (where deep cutting was welcomed as a practical defence against heat evaporation).

Harry Powell of the Whitefriars Glasshouse, addressing the Society of Arts in 1906, stressed that the object of cutting was to give expression to one of the metal's essential qualities—inherent brilliancy—'without obscuring the form given to the glass by the glass blower's breath'. One result was an abundance of tall, tapering vessels. Early in the period, for example, the classical onochoe was elongated into a decanter with inverted pyriform body narrowing to a flat foot ring, at first sometimes linked by a brief stem. Above, a long, narrow neck with a petal rim supported a conspicuously long-shouldered stopper.

Some firms such as the Edinburgh and Leith Glasshouse developed in drinking glasses the slender straw stem, finely drawn from the bowl; even among the period's abundant frilly vases in cheap ruby glass there was a liking for simple funnel or flower-bud shapes. Many flower-engraved Edwardian jugs modified the long-favoured cylinder shape to a taller, tapering outline, very narrow at the lip and with a handle set low above the swelling base. Informal and even asymmetrical outlines were approved, in table centre epergnes, for example, and in 'bunched-up napkin' finger-bowls.

Where Edwardians looked beyond traditional deep wheel-cutting the ornament was mainly in one of several styles of shallower wheel-engraving. Here there is much to enjoy, the clear thin glass proving remarkably light and strong. These tall, slender table vessels, plain or in waved or fluted outline, were well suited by the period's upward spiralling plant engravings and graceful arabesques. Here too, of

D

course, the collector finds mainly a fresh Edwardian impetus to technical skills already established.

Rock crystal engraving, for example, is especially brilliant. Wheel-engraved ornament usually appears as softly opaque lines, but here the deep engraving is polished so that the whole surface shows a watery gleam. Brierley Hill and Stourbridge Museums display fine examples. Rock crystal glass was launched in Victorian England by the Stourbridge firm of Thomas Webb where William Fritsche, 1853–1924, from Bohemia, proved to be one of the finest engravers ever to come to this country. Fritsche and his contemporary F. E. Kny had settled in England a generation earlier but three Kny sons continued the craft, including the brilliant Ludvig who worked for Webb and Corbett, and notable examples of this glass came from English crafts-men at Stevens and Williams, Brierley Hill. The technique was con-tinued into the 1920s but the fashion began to wane by about 1908 when it became known simply as bright polished engraving. One important result, noted by Wilkinson, was the wide success of glass engraving through the first quarter of this century, with the Stourbridge area employing over 300. Much rock crystal glass went to America.

Ornament deeply wheel-engraved into the glass was known as intaglio engraving. W. J. Hodgetts, for example, worked for the Stevens and Williams firm at Brierley Hill for over 40 years until retirement in 1929, winning a reputation for botanically correct flower intaglios in clear glass of many different colours. An interesting deve-lopment was intaglio cutting from the underside of a glass, such as a paperweight, so that the ornament appeared to be in relief. But in more ambitious work the engraved ornament stood out in true relief. This was crystal cameo engraving, produced by Stevens and Williams from 1906.

Even this, however, is not to be confused with the period's most prestigious carving on cased glass, known as the glass cameo, reflecting an Establishment love of familiar neo-classicism. Once glassmen had rediscovered the ancient technique of fusing or casing glass in thin layers of different colours, clear or opaque, one within another, they had a fascinating material not only for obvious deep cutting but for carving in delicate relief. In the glass cameo an outer casing of opaque white could be carved down to an innermost layer in a contrasting dark tone, in the manner of the classic Portland vase. Here again the first triumphs had come in the previous century, to such men as John Northwood, 1836–1902, but collectors may observe a wide range of Edwardian work. Northwood's son, another John, 1870–1960, and a nephew William also contributed to the craft. The Northwoods worked as decorators on their own and then for the firm of Stevens and Williams, while the renowned Woodall brothers, Thomas, 1849–1926, and George, 1850–1925, made cameo glass for Thomas Webb and Son.

Frederick Carder, one-time Northwood pupil, described how Northwood carved his cameos in the fragile glass with hardened steel tools one-eighth to one-sixteenth of an inch in diameter, their long triangular points giving three cutting edges; he worked with a scraping action towards his protected left thumb. Collectors notice the pure white of Northwood cameos in contrast to the hint of blue in the Woodall white, especially effective where it is carved away to a filmy translucence over the customary dark blue or chocolate tone of the underlying background glass.

The cameo's success was brief, killed by effective Bohemian imitations more simply painted in enamels—understandable enough in view of the current success of *pâte-sur-pâte* and 'Limoges' porcelain ornaments. But more cameo work was made in my period than is sometimes realized. Owen Gibbon in the *Pottery Gazette*, January 1908, declared: 'No more noble ornament can be conceived in a room than a fine well-designed and artistically executed cameo vase ... having a gem-like quality which is truly precious.'

Signatures *T. & G. Woodall* and *G. Woodall* usually signify their early work; *Geo. Woodall* more often a twentieth-century piece. Woodall work was on show at the 1908 Franco-British exhibition and even after he retired from Webb's in 1911, George Woodall continued making cameos at home. Prices for a few such as his *Dancing Hours* were in hundreds of pounds. In 1907 the *Connoisseur* review of work at the Wahliss Galleries praised Woodall's typical classical figures—Diana and Endymion, Hebe and the like—for the effects of light and shade, soft perspective and bold relief, rounded limb and gossamer drapery. In *Aphrodite*, for example, the thin brittle glass was sculpted to suggest waves washing lightly over the figure's out-stretched limbs and flowing hair, and this sense of life and movement is much in the spirit of his period. He was considered successful even with portraits and such commemorative work as a vase with Polar scenes marking the Shackleton 1907 expedition.

It is important to realize that cameo effects on ornaments and tableware in thinner layers of glass were extensively aided by acid and engraving wheels to cut away unwanted glass. Such cameos were made on a considerable scale by Webb and Sons (some marked *Webb Gem Cameo*), Stevens and Williams and other firms such as the Richardsons of Wordsley, employing altogether well over a hundred men. As many as four or six layers of colour may be revealed in different details of a flower or fruit pattern. But two-colour work is effective, such as opaque white 'opal' over clear pale ruby, or the reverse of this, with clear colour over a white background, known as soft relief or *dolce relievo* cameo. Craftsmen whose names are known included Harry Davies, 1869–1942, who worked also on Wedgwood ware, Northwood's assistant W. J. Hodgetts and the Woodalls' assistant J. T. Fereday. Daniel Pearce, d. 1907, and Lionel, d. 1926, formed a father-and-son partnership making many cameo scent bottles and Chinese-inspired vases.

At this time the commonest use of acid on glass was in simple etched decoration. It was applied over designs cut through a bituminous acid-resistant mask on the glass to put minor bands and sprigs on much-handled everyday glassware such as carafe sets. But more complicated effects achieved with cleverly controlled hydrofluoric acid fascinated some art glass decorators prepared to take the risks involved. Acid polishing, lead free, came later.

Elaborate cutting and engraving in clear flint glass and the coloured layers of cased glass were the Edwardian glassman's main ornamental skills but Powell himself took glass decoration even further. E. M. Elville in *English Table Glass* has described how he introduced eye-pleasing contrasts by varying the thickness of a vessel's walls to 'concentrate the transmitted light in regions of brilliance'. He was fascinated by the bold, expressive ways that the glass could be shaped and ornamented at the furnace mouth: Davis and Middlemas considered his slender plastic shapes, chastely decorated, comparable with any in Europe. Powell mentioned in his book that Whitefriars tableware had been represented in almost every exhibition with an arts and crafts section from 1851 to 1914 and Hugh Wakefield, too, noted that Powell's firm 'tended increasingly to represent an intellectual and purist attitude towards glass making'.

Henry Tooth put it all clearly to J. F. Blacker in about 1905: 'The Bohemian glass with its crude tints and obtrusive decorations was valued only so long as the "wholeness" of effect which we now look for in all well-furnished rooms was disregarded; but ... now it is almost valueless.'

The period suffered its losses, of course. According to Dudley Westropp flint-glass making in Ireland ceased in the 1890s. In Scotland, Clutha art glass was interestingly original in primitive fluid form, uneven texture and smoky colours, sometimes with a glint of metallic aventurine. But this was last made by James Couper and Sons of Glasgow in 1900, and then to the designs of George Walton, no longer those of Christopher Dresser, although the firm continued making decorative wares until 1911. This is not to be confused with the Cluthra glass developed by Carder in America.

Brilliant technician Frederick Carder, 1863–1963, took off for America in 1903 with another half century of work ahead of him, but not before he had helped to develop the translucent satin-surfaced jade glass in the stone's many gentle hues such as 'Rosaline'. This was made by Stevens and Williams throughout my period (and sometimes used as casing over white for engraved decoration). Another success was the moss agate glass he invented with John Northwood, streaked with soft colours and cleverly lined with soda glass that with heat would produce crackled effects.

The firm of H. C. Richardson and Sons, too, in 1905 advertised their matt-surfaced Ceonix glass with the boast that it owed its beauty to the metal itself and its graceful shaping. There was no applied decoration, just 'beautiful erratic marble effects in pale soft green tints'.

Those concerned with Edwardian coloured glass tend to concentrate on such contrasting Continental leaders as Gallé and Lalique or the American Tiffany workshops. But so much craft skill has been involved in handling glass with metallic oxide colours that it is scarcely surprising to find many English successes, including revived Venetian techniques prompted by the Earls Court Italian exhibition in 1904. West Midlands glass, cut, engraved and coloured, is represented by collections at Brierley Hill and Stourbridge under Mr Charles Hajdamach, keeper of Glass and Fine Arts for Dudley Metropolitan Borough.

The time of marvelling had passed perhaps. Glass cased by fusing colour within colour had become commonplace as had the minor wonder of colour varied within a single vessel by repeated selective applications of heat at the furnace 'glory hole'. Webb, under licence, made Queen's Burmese glass, for example, glowing with colours that shaded from greenish-yellow to warm pink. This was opaque but from about 1900 Thomas Webb and Stevens and Williams also made sparkling three-colour Alexandrite glass—amber-to-rose-to-blue.

By another well-established skill trinket glasses were 'quilted' with air bubbles within the thickness of the glass, a Benjamin Richardson patent followed by various refinements. This was an elaboration of cased glass. The first layer of white glass was given an intaglio-patterned surface from a mould and the air-filled hollows covered by translucent coloured glass, often with the surface shine muted by acid to a satin sheen. At its most elaborate the quilted glass was covered with a further layer of white glass and this was acid-etched as a cameo against the light-catching 'mother-of-pearl' background. Some splendid gilding by Jules Barbe was given this quilted ground.

Much coloured glass was used for flower vases, including the elaborate table centres with silver or electro-plated branching stands described as 'the new style' by Mappin and Webb in 1904–5. Their long trumpets of glass were often twisted with fine threads of glass (another process improved by Richardson) or the Edwardians' favourite blobby trailings. Individual vases appeared in many tall slender shapes with asymmetrical rim outlines. A. Stanier, for example, working for Stuart and Sons, devised some attractive designs around 1905. Here trails of glass rose vertically from the vessel's base and appeared to criss-cross as they encircled the everted rim. These sold as the 'Ribbonette' decoration, described by the Army and Navy Stores as 'delicate grass green coils on best English flint-glass'.

The 'old-fashioned' urge to make glass imitate other materials continued too, as in Thomas Webb's opaque, whitish glass, acid-patterned in relief and tinted to suggest its name of 'carved ivory'. This prompted Japanese shapes etched and gilded with dragonflies and the like. The Victorian patent by a Londoner, E. Varnish, for sealing untarnishing silver within the glass was followed by more complex notions, even to patterning the glass in metal by electro-deposit.

The silvered iridescent glass called Silveria was a John Northwood II development, of about 1900, for Stevens and Williams, using an ancient technique. A gather of lightly tinted clear glass was blown to shape and, while hot, was rolled on the glassman's flat slab or marver to pick up a layer of silver foil, sealed into the glass by a further dipping into the pot of hot glass. A brilliant variant of this technique, also on view at Stourbridge, sealed the metallic foil between the layers of glass before expanding the vessel on the blowing iron so that the stretched foil shattered into tiny shining fragments. Other fancy glass of the period glittered with metal filings or fragments of mica or many-coloured glass chippings.

This was for the popular end of the trade. Much cheap glass was shaped and patterned by being blown into moulds, such as the many ripple-surfaced bowls and vases bearing the white enamel paintings of children at play: much of this 'Mary Gregory' glass came from Bohemia. Obviously blown-moulded glass may be much more recent than its shape suggests and this applies especially to all the extremely collectable and still abundant ruby or cranberry glass.

The best ruby glass was cased—a layer of clear glass within a layer of the costly ruby colour obtained from gold chloride—for traditional deep geometric cutting. In one price-cutting method for wine glasses the ruby glass was blown as a long tube so that lengths could be cut and cup-shaped for casing inside clear glass bowls, relying on heat for perfect fusion. But the collector finds far more merely tinted with a minimal quantity of colour to hide blemishes in the cheap ware made by minor firms. Some clear glass was surface-flashed—just dipped quickly in the pot of tinted molten glass before reheating and blowing to shape; some merely part-stained after shaping, with brush-painted, heat-fixed colour. Added details that give a glass its character—feet, frills and trailings—were often of clear glass to avoid the difficulty of colour matching.

Among Edwardian lamps, for example, collectors may find ruby glass in all qualities, cased, blown-moulded and pressed. Victorians thought pressed glass an improvement on the old blown-moulded technique. A smooth-surfaced plunger forced the hot glass into the mould, achieving cheap and reasonably sharp imitations of cut glass. In clear glass, clear ruby, opaque turquoise and so on, it supplied Edwardians with many workaday tablewares and trinkets including coronation and other commemorative souvenirs.

Collectors of boots, baskets, spill vases and the like must realize that old moulds (some with Victorian marks) were brought out again whenever opportunity offered. Some of the most popular scarcely resemble glass, selling as vitro-porcelain. The name slag-glass for the marbled blackberry-and-white ware derived from the glassy slag from molten steel included in its mix. Makers of pressed glass whose marks are known included H. Greener of Sunderland, Sowerbys and George Davidson of Gateshead, W. H. Heppell of Newcastle, Butler Tate and Company, Edward Moore and Company and John Ford. Davidson and Company included colour-shaded ornaments.

Much of all this is as impossible to date as the clever little curiosities —walking sticks, bells and so on—in cheap ruby and white-striped glass still good for a laugh around the turn of the century. Even those primitive looking beehive doorstops in cool green bottle glass were still made, as witnessed by an occasional coronation motif in pressed clay trapped within the glass where more usually the ornament is a flower shape composed of air bubbles. Some of these domes were made by the Wakefield firm of J. Kilner and Sons but few are found with any marks.

It would be unfair to this period to omit one branch of the glass trade then still extremely important, although so soon worked to death in suburban hall-door and fanlight. Many Edwardian designer-craftsmen were still proud to list stained glass among their achievements, such as Crane, Heywood Sumner and the influential Glasgow

[45]

school. Margaret Macdonald, for example, devised many leaded glass panels for her husband's light fittings and Ann Macbeth could work in glass as successfully as in appliqué needlework.

Here, too, technical developments played a part both in stamping the window quarries and in colouring the glass. Harry Powell noted many experiments, resulting, for instance, in orange glass, its colour derived from selenium, exhibited in 1906. The firm made glass in 1913 for Liverpool Cathedral and St John's Cathedral, New York. And in St Paul's Cathedral even discarded glass chippings proved useful for the mosaics made by the firm to designs by Sir William Richmond, completed in 1904.

Stained glass advertisement in The Studio, *Winter number 1900–1*

1. Upright cabinet designed by Charles Rennie Mackintosh. This shows how the complexity of curves associated with his early work gave way to severely rectilinear forms, expressed even in the cut-out squares decorating the cabinet doors. Colour contrasts are introduced in the glass and mirror detail of the bowed recess and there is further enrichment with mother of pearl. Height 66 in. About 1905. *Courtesy of Sotheby's Belgravia.*

2. Armchair by C. R. Mackintosh, also dating to the period when his work was at its peak. This was designed for the music room at *Hous'hill*, home of Miss Cranston, who is remembered today for her long appreciation of this difficult perfectionist and for her tearooms where he could express his concern for the 'total environment' in his designs. The chair is of stained wood, the oval insets of mauve glass. Height 47 in. About 1905. *Courtesy of Sotheby's Belgravia.*

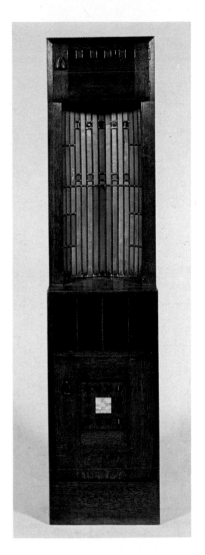

3. Interesting techniques in coloured glass vases of the 1900s. *Left:* in green glass cased with white and acid-etched with a woodland scene. This is almost certainly by J. B. Hill, 1850–1928, who worked at the Northwood decorating workshops and later for Stevens and Williams, Brierley Hill. Height 7⅝ in. *Centre:* a development of the Silveria technique, the amber glass covered with flakes of silver leaf and cased with crystal. Probably by Stevens and Williams. Height 13¾ in. *Right:* Silveria glass vase decorated by the technique by John Northwood II at the Stevens and Williams glassworks. Height 8⅝ in. *All courtesy of the Council House, Stourbridge.*

4. Late examples of William de Morgan's work, dating to the early 20th century when this artist-novelist was in partnership with Frank Iles and Charles and Fred Passenger at Sands End Pottery, Fulham. By then the decoration was executed by his assistants but he continued to be responsible for all the characteristic two-dimensional design. *Courtesy of the Victoria and Albert Museum.*

5. Bottle vase showing the lustrous brilliance characteristic of Pilkington's Lancastrian Pottery. This is painted by the firm's chief designer Gordon Forsyth and marked with his four-scythes rebus. Height 15¼ in. Date-coded for 1909. *Courtesy of Sotheby's Belgravia.*

6. Jewellery designed by Charles Robert Ashbee and made by his Guild of Handicraft. The ship is of enamelled gold set with opal and hung with amethysts. About 1903. The pendant and chain are in enamelled gold set with chrysoprases. *Courtesy of the Victoria and Albert Museum.*

7. Necklace, maker unknown, but suggesting the style of C. R. Ashbee. This is in silver-gilt, decorated with translucent enamel and set with opals. About 1900. *Courtesy of the Victoria and Albert Museum.*

8. Royal Worcester vases painted by two of the period's leading porcelain decorators. The pair, 16 in. tall, were ornamented by Walter Powell, who first worked for the important decorator James Hadley. Date-coded for 1911. The 20½ in. vase is by John Stinton, one of a family of porcelain painters, who worked for the Grainger firm before the two Worcester factories combined. He specialised in vases and plaques painted with cattle scenes. Date-coded for 1912. *Courtesy of Sotheby's Belgravia.*

6

Pottery

EDWARDIAN potters have left us a bewildering array of collectable work. Their ornamental porcelains may appear as graciously formidable as the Edwardian ladies who adored them but their homelier earthenwares are completely approachable, sometimes mocking with bizarre design, more often charming with inventive ornament and heart-warming colour. These range from the art potters' salt-glazed, 'drain pipe' stonewares through matt-surfaced jasper and basalts to the refined earthenwares given the courtesy name of stone chinas and semi-porcelains, and the architectural potters' warm terracottas.

Some were named for their surface glazes. These included the metallic lustres, the glowing black-coffee rockingham brown and the majolicas and faiences associated only distantly with the early Italian earthenwares transformed by costly opaque-white tin glaze.

Such contemporary commentators as J. F. Blacker in *Nineteenth Century Ceramic Art*, researched through my period, emphasize the important part played by many major manufacturers from the Ridgways and Meakins of Hanley and Tunstall to the Malings of Newcastle, from the Bells' Glasgow pottery to Bristol. All and many more served Edwardian homes with ornaments and conservatory pots, tablewares and toilet sets. Such giants as Worcester, Mintons and Copelands were so widely involved with porcelains that it has seemed best to consider them in the next chapter. But here Mintons must be given credit for introducing to other potters the soft, heavily leaded 'English majolica' colour glazes that glowed with extraordinary richness on relief-moulded cane-coloured wares and on the white body used by Wedgwood for particularly striking effects.

The range of commercial shape and pattern was remarkable. As the Longton firm of Charles Allerton and Son told Blacker in about 1903, they had needed perhaps half a dozen cup shapes 25 years before but 'today we must have about 50 shapes, or we should get left behind . . . we are continually adding new shapes and decorations'.

Collectors can see in some of these products a natural continuation of

[47]

long-loved workaday ornament, from primitive mocha 'moss' patterns and banded wares to gold-washed 'copper' lustres. The Allerton firm, for example, were still making these gold lustres in early shapes, and 'silver' lustre too despite a 700 per cent rise in the cost of the necessary platinum. Some popular wares are especially interesting to collectors as coronation souvenirs though these cost the potters dearly. Being prepared in advance they were printed with what proved to be the wrong date when the king's illness necessitated postponement.

Other popular wares were already in vogue with collectors, as noted by Blacker among the Sunderland sailor pieces—frog mugs and the like daubed with the cheapest pink-gold lustres—and this is a reminder that collectors must be prepared for the confusion of reproductions. Old moulds were available and already the pottery firm of William Kent was advertising 'old Staffordshire figures' among its specialities. Edwardian mantlepiece spaniels may declare their date with supercilious glassy eyes but many an Edwardian Staffordshire portrait figure still passes as mid-Victorian, from highwayman to Tam o' Shanter, although glossy Bohemian fairings had shaken the cottagers' long affection for such companionable heroes and villains, apart from a few Boer War leaders.

Another pitfall for the unwary may be an Edwardian picture potlid although this can be recognized, according to Cyril Williams-Wood, by changes in body and glaze and 'a marked deterioration in the quality of the printing'. Here the real teasers for beginner-collectors were issued later still, but collectors must step carefully among Edwardian ceramics that seriously sought to recapture later eighteenth-century glories. At the end of the chapter I give some marks, and these are often helpful. The Wedgwood firm, for example, included *England* from 1891 and *Made in England* from about 1910 on the queen's ware reintroduced under John E. Godwin from 1902, in fine shapes and ornament based on Georgian originals. Their traditional decoration in jasper ware was high in Edwardian affections too, stimulating the opening of the Wedgwood Museum in 1906. 'Replicas of the "Wine" and "Water" vases in Black Basalt Ware' were advertised by the company in *The Connoisseur* in Edwardian days.

With some other fine craftsmanship more serious problems arise. In renowned Leeds creamware, for example, traditional shapes were still produced in our period bearing the old *Leeds Pottery* marks. The principal maker was James Senior, using some of the original moulds; when he died in 1909 the business went to his son. W. W. Slee, often associated with these fine wares, was an antique dealer who merely handled them. Another important maker was J. T. Morton who worked for Senior, 1907–10, and subsequently on his own account, making fine quality pierced wares but without the Leeds mark.

But it is individual skill, original rather than imitative, that attracts many collectors to this period. Their quest is the work of artist-potters who felt impelled by the sheer ugliness of much ill-controlled industrialization to express themselves in exciting new ways. Continuing the late Victorian arts and crafts movement, these men and women prepared the public to appreciate the full self-expression of the modern studio potter.

It is easy now to see the important outside influences at work, especially Oriental, traceable in design, material and ornament. But many of those early art potters appeared at the time to be wholly absorbed by a personal pleasure in contact with colour and clay. Basically the collector here seeks out work of three groups. There were those who consciously found new subtleties of shape and texture and ornamental motif while using the country potter's ancient slipwares and salt-glazed stonewares. There were the country potters themselves, by then fully aroused by the aesthetes and breaking away from traditional plain functionalism with naive designs and uses of colours. And there were the glaze enthusiasts whose chemical formulae and sophisticated furnace techniques transformed timeless academic shapes with their new intensities of colour and lustrous sheen before legal health precautions limited their scope. Their wide success is indicated by the range of distinctively Edwardian pottery already being sought by astute collectors.

These early art potters pursued their intellectual, consciously aesthetic aims in extremely varied conditions, and by no means all achieved the modern studio potter's self-sufficiency. Some worked at least partly under the aegis of a major firm, such as Alfred and Louise Powell who established a painting school at Wedgwoods, and Tinworth and Marshall then still giving impetus to the art pottery at Doultons of Lambeth. The Powells first exhibited their work in 1905, designed and painted by them and made at Etruria. At their own London pottery they made tin-glazed earthenware suitable for painted ornament. A typical two-handled vase, 18 inches high, has a hawk chasing a heron through blossoming boughs among a flurry of small birds and petals.

The Doulton factory art rooms, in collaboration with the Lambeth School of Art, involved over a hundred student artists. Using essentially simple, direct salt-glazed stonewares these men and women developed a range of decorative techniques, incising, carving, sprigging, stamping, colouring and slip trailing the coarse ware. E. A. Barber, writing in about 1906, noted that this art stoneware could

[49]

include a combination of processes. 'Surrounding the zones of panels of scratched decoration . . . are bands of coloured enamels, outlined and carved designs and bossed or jewelled work . . . ' But all these artists relied on professional turners, throwers and furnace men to shape and fire their vessels. Similarly the London Central School of Arts and Crafts merely decorated commercially prepared pots until 1926.

Doulton stonewares at this period included light-coloured silicon ware with a slight smear glaze over its carved or perforated ornament, sometimes with touches of gilding, and 'black leather' silicon with a Cromwellian air. Doulton's china ware was given a textured net surface with fabric pressed into the soft clay before firing. Even leaves might be pressed on the clay in another of their art wares but perhaps the most challenging was marquetery ware with geometrical patterns formed in a mosaic of coloured clays.

Today there is a remarkable demand for animal scenes incised freehand in the wet stoneware surface by Hannah Barlow, for example, who kept her own small zoo. By Edwardian days Mark V. Marshall had an international reputation for modelling, including grotesques, and John Broad was actively modelling in stoneware and terracotta. George Tinworth, mentioned by Desmond Eyles as Doulton's first 'arty interloper' of 1866, 'continued to be lionized as the "grand old man" of the Lambeth studios'. But already by then Doulton's Harry Simeon was looking ahead to the austere mood of the 1920s.

Collectors of workaday stonewares note that the Doulton firm in 1913 absorbed the Lambeth pottery of James Stiff and Sons, makers of collectable 'Gothic' water filters as well as terracotta garden ornaments.

The period saw a slow decline in demand for art stonewares and expansion in ornaments of Doulton's Burslem earthenwares and bone china. These included impasto, painted with clay slip in slight relief before firing, and a variety of 'faience'. The Doulton firm applied this term to ware of a natural clay tone in contrast to normal commercial white wares. The firm's faience jugs and vases were lavishly catalogued by the Army and Navy Stores, beside Worcester-Hadley faience painted with irises and daffodils.

Other long-proved ornament continued, such as majolica glazes and 'toby' items in the brown-ware tradition with figures and country scenes in relief showing whitish against backgrounds of dark brown or blue. C. J. Noke went to Burslem as a modeller, becoming art director in 1914. His bowls and plaques in Rembrandt ware won praise in 1908 for their rugged look, the ornament, such as shadowy heads, painted underglaze in layers of coloured slips. Quaint stylized heads in the *art nouveau* manner are also to be found on Noke's harder Holbein ware.

Such was the spirit of the time that other firms, too, began to offer studio conditions to decorative artists from the increasingly popular schools of art and design: in 1908, for example, the *Art Journal* commended the studio work of the Lancastrian Pottery where 'Mr Burton has gathered a band of young artists', the only stipulation being that ornament must be in keeping with the vessel's shape. At Burmantofts, Leeds, 'Mr Holroyd converted a strictly utilitarian business into an art pottery'.

Mintons had had a London art studio briefly in the 1870s. This was not reopened after a disastrous fire, but a reminder of the mood continued into my period in the huge colourful birds and fishes painted by Austrian W. Mussill on ornamental wares using a heavy barbotine (kaolin clay paste) technique. Mintons' *art nouveau* Secessionist ware, moulded and slip trailed, was introduced by Leon Solon in 1902, taking its name from the Viennese group with shared ideals of a new unacademic style. Many of the fluid *art nouveau* shapes were decorated in richly coloured flowing glazes including browns, yellow-greens and cold blues. In the mood of the day Wardle and Company of Hanley became the Wardle Art Pottery Company in 1910.

Among those most nearly achieving the modern ideals of studio craftsmen-potters were the Martin brothers. Robert Wallace Martin, 1843-1923, trained as a sculptor but developed his skill with salt-glazed stoneware in C. J. C. Bailey's factory at Fulham under the artist-potter J. C. Cazin. Walter and Edwin Martin worked for a time at Doulton's before the brothers, including Charles as sales manager, set up their own pottery.

Martinwares are so well known, including grotesques in the Gothic gargoyle tradition, that it is enough here to recall how their work mellowed after their contact with the shapes and glazes of Continental art pottery under Japanese influence at the Paris 1900 exhibition. A less familiar source of stoneware figures early this century was the husband and wife partnership Harold (1877–1945) and Phoebe Stabler at Hammersmith. The Poole Pottery under the partnership of Carter, Stabler and Adams later reissued some of these.

Country potteries, traditional source of salt-glazed stonewares and brown earthenwares, themselves became part of this art-conscious movement when aesthetes sought out their useful wares, especially slip-decorated pots. Some, such as the brown stoneware potters of Denby and Brampton, Derbyshire, merely continued long-favoured decorative items. These included puzzle jugs in stoneware and buff-toned terracotta, small animal figures and the familiar Brampton jugs with country scenes in relief, heavy mask spouts and greyhound handles. But many another country potter was prompted to make showier, costlier wares.

Today collectors may be surprised at the twentieth-century date of many a Derbyshire rockingham-brown toby jug, West Country baking dish or Yorkshire chimney ornament, as well as the ubiquitous motto ornaments and tablewares. Combing, rouletting, sprigging and inlaid patterns in contrasting clays continued until the 1920s at a great number of minor potteries, alongside plain workaday crocks, from huge rhubarb pots and Derbyshire clouts (big mugs) to bird whistles. Other potters sought artistic effects with colour innovations, aided by the colour supplier A. F. Wenger of the Helvetia Works, Hanley. At the Wrecclesham Pottery, Farnham, for example, P. C. D. Brears noted art wares with dark green, iridescent glaze on white slip over the basic red earthenware, made around 1900 by Absalon Harris, this Farnham greenware (sold by Liberty's) continuing in production to 1914. He has drawn attention to the fact that such potters as Harris of Farnham and Isaac Burton of Halifax provided artistic shapes in red ware covered with white slip for amateurs to decorate in incised patterns, subsequently fired by the potteries.

From Rye in Sussex to Kirkcaldy in Fife attempts were being made to meet the fashionable demand by ornamenting traditional shapes whether with 'Etruscan' decoration or equally self-conscious rusticity. For example, the Rye Belle Vue Pottery under the Mitchell family loaded their brown wares with naturally coloured hops. This firm also made the Sussex pig jug with a loose head forming a cup for drinking celebratory 'hogsheads of beer'. More pigs came from the Fife Pottery, Gallatown, near Kirkcaldy under widely-travelled Robert Heron, 1870–1906. Here soft, easily crazed earthenware pots, and eventually large pieces, were lavishly painted with thistles, roses, mottoes and so on by a group of artists encouraged by the Grosvenor family of Wemyss Castle. Art director of this Wemyss ware was Karel Nekola (d. 1915) who occasionally signed a boldly painted plaque. London supplies were exclusive to Thomas Goode and Company. Eventually Nekola's son took the firm's moulds to the Bovey Tracey Pottery, Devon.

In Essex the aesthetes concentrated on the Castle Hedingham pottery where schoolmaster-mystic, Edward Bingham, transformed his father's workaday establishment, producing a range of intriguingly idiosyncratic vessels, wall plates, candlesticks and so on. This continued as the Essex Art-Pottery Company until 1905 under Bingham's son, but the unwary collector may be misled by the copying of primitive ornament and inscriptions and occasional early dates on such vessels as tygs, mugs and puzzle jugs.

Bingham's experimental colour glazing was dominated by fine blues and greens, browns and greys but his work is especially sought by collectors because of his absorption with Essex history. His famous Essex jug, for instance, was sold accompanied by an explanation of its ornament. Other items were themselves inscribed at length. This was, of course, self-conscious art pottery work: some pieces were marked *East Anglian Art Pottery* or *Royal Art Pottery Works* as well as with Bingham's name or initials. But contemporary records leave the impression of a contented family pottery set in a country cottage garden.

In the West Country Edwin Beer Fishley, 1861–1911, continued the Fremington pottery until his death. Much of his work was in traditional country style—brown clay richly colour-glazed, notably in a mottled, iridescent dark green. This well suited his candlesticks and puzzle jugs and lidless cadogan teapots (filled through a spiralling base hole in the ancient Oriental manner) that he sold to Barnstable's summer visitors. But more ambitious sgraffito work was noted by Blacker. In this, before firing, a layer of whitish slip over the brown ware was cut away where not required, leaving the pattern against the brown background.

Using the same fine clay another potter's son, C. H. Brannam, 1855–1937, and his sons won a high reputation for the Litchdon Pottery, Barnstable, with simple well-thrown Barum ware. Here, too, decoration was in white slip over a red earthenware body in the old sgraffito technique but with laborious care to meet the critical demands of the art market and in particular the London dealers Howell and James. Late work included blue, green and yellow slip ornament under a clear lead glaze. Blessed by a royal warrant from Queen Victoria the ware was retailed by Liberty's until the 1930s. In style it followed the fashions of the period, eventually acquiring a somewhat Celtic flavour. Edwardian advertisements offered 'special terms for bazaars'.

The art potter of this region whose experiments in form were sometimes condemned even at the time as excessively quaint was the self-taught Sir Edmund Elton at the Sunflower Pottery, Clevedon. But Elton won many exhibition gold medals and continued production for over 40 years until his death in 1920. His decoration ranged from coloured and modelled slips to metallic glazes such as crackled silver, and he followed current fashion for perforated ornaments. He devised his own kilns, wheel and fine colouring, such as blended blues and greens, reds and purples, violet and grey.

At this art-conscious period even the Watcombe and Torquay terra-cotta companies felt the urge to add touches of colour to the relief moulding on their satisfying, warm-toned ware. Much was holiday souvenir work brightly painted with flowers, dismissed by Blacker because 'mere oil painting on terracotta is outside the art of the potter'. He preferred the designs of fish and seaweeds in brown and green underglaze colouring applied in the thin clay paste of barbotine painting. He considered the large Watcombe vases to be in a class apart, skilfully painted with birds and flowers on a white or dark ground.

Such work had proved popular at Aller Vale near Newton Abbot. At the beginning of this period Watcombe joined the Aller Vale Art Pottery Company to form the Royal Aller Vale and Watcombe Pottery Company so that the word *Royal* appears in Edwardian marks. There were then as many as 60 employees, including art students and local boys in training. Their popular crocus vases are still to be found, the flowers rising from the bulbs up the sides of tall narrow-waisted shapes. London's Army and Navy Stores made a considerable feature of their Devonshire art pottery. Inevitably in such an area, as with many a country pottery, such as nearby Longpark from 1905, cheap motto ware was popular, bearing a town name perhaps or a phrase such as *Be aisy with the cream*. This might be lettered in slip or incised around flowers or a simple rustic scene.

Christopher Dresser's art pottery designs came too early for this survey, as Linthorpe near Middlesbrough closed in 1899. But the pottery was long remembered for using flowing, unpredictable glazes as sole ornament on some pieces, then an exciting concept to art potters. These glazes proved difficult to control in firing and produced spontaneous, unrepeatable patterns.

Henry Tooth began his career in pottery at Linthorpe before establish-ing the Bretby Art Pottery, Woodville, Derbyshire, in partnership with William Ault. Here much work was deliberately imitative, suggesting, for instance, the period's boldly riveted art metal work. Such names as 'copperette', 'carved bamboo', 'cloisonné', explain themselves. Ashtrays were popular in imitative designs: typically a leaf has biscuits and fruit lying on it.

The firm continued as Tooth and Company after Ault established his own pottery a few miles away at Swadlincote in 1887, continuing through Edwardian days. Here, too, glaze ornament was developed in splashed, striated and broken colour effects. Blacker noted toby jugs and grotesques. Gamages described Ault faience as 'the last word in Art Pottery' in 1913, offering, for example, tea wares, trinket sets and a fish-shaped hot water bottle.

28 and 29. Further examples of notable Knox design in Liberty's Tudric pewter. The vase of about 1906–9, shaped as an inverted cone with curved sides, is set within three handles that also form the base, their starkly-plain outlines being in striking contrast to the elaborate interlacing plant forms above. The pewter tea service, *below*, on a matching tray dates to about 1903–4. It has been suggested that Knox drew some of his inspiration from contact with Christopher Dresser, who surely would have approved of the bold, spare lines of these pleasantly functional vessels. All made for Liberty's by W. H. Haseler of Birmingham. *All courtesy of the Victoria and Albert Museum.*

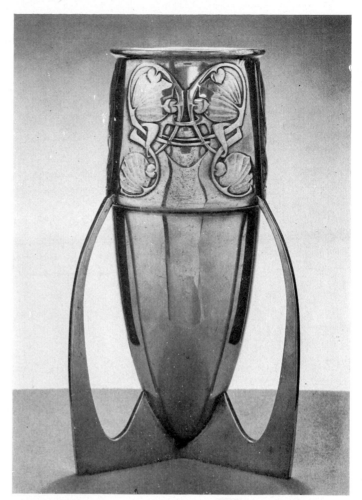

30. *Birth of Aphrodite*, a glass cameo plaque by George Woodall in white against a background in a dark amber tone. The extremely difficult cameo technique was evolved by Victorian glass decorators determined to copy the classic Portland vase. Layers of glass, dark and milky white, were fused together (cased) and the white partially removed. Acid, using a resist process, and wheel-and-emery engraving could shorten this tedious work, but for such a prestige piece all the delicate detail had to be hand carved with hardened steel tools. George Woodall proved perhaps the most successful exponent: his signature here—*Geo Woodall*—indicating a date around 1900. It is interesting to compare this with Birks' pâte-sur-pâte work for Mintons in fig. 60. *Private collection. Photograph by courtesy of the Council House, Stourbridge.*

32. (*Opposite page*) *Left*: vase with blown-moulded ornament accentuated by cutting in *art nouveau* stylized leaf and flower pattern. *Centre*: acid-etched and cut ornament based on the Indian cone pattern (stopper perhaps not original). *Right*: vase of dark green glass decorated with flower sprays by a silver deposit technique. Made at Wordsley and probably shown at the opening of the Wordsley School of Art, 1899. *Left and centre, courtesy of the Council House, Stourbridge; right, courtesy of Brierley Hill Glass Museum.*

31. Delicate ornament on sherry and champagne glass bowls, cut
stems and feet. *Left to right*: bright polished *art nouveau* engraving;
pillars and festoons by William Fritsche; garlands and parrots signed
H. *Palme* and acid-marked *Webb*; ruby-cased bowl, cut and acid-etched.
*Left and left-centre, courtesy of the Council House, Stourbridge; right-centre
and right, courtesy of Brierley Hill Glass Museum.*

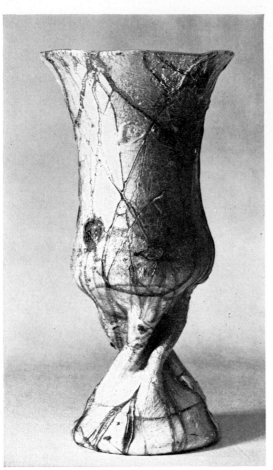

33. Highly-skilled, casual-looking twisted shape in a Silveria vase made by Stevens and Williams of Brierley Hill. The glass has been cased to enclose silver foil and is further decorated with green glass trailing. Stevens and Williams mark on base. Height 12½ in. About 1900. *Courtesy of the Victoria and Albert Museum.*

34. Vase made and marked by Stevens and Williams where W. J. Hodgetts was noted for such deep intaglio engraving. Here the ornament is rendered particularly effective by use of cased glass—pale olive green cased with a pinkish plum colour. Dated 1901. Height 12 in. *Courtesy of the Victoria and Albert Museum.*

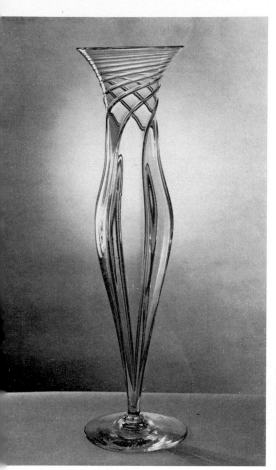

35. Glass vase in the period's favourite slender shape exploiting the material's limpid, flowing beauty. Long trails of glass have been arranged with great skill to encircle the mouth of the clear glass vessel and continue down the swelling body to the narrow base. Made by A. Stanier at the Stourbridge firm of Stuart & Sons. About 1905. *Courtesy of the Victoria and Albert Museum.*

36. Early 20th-century bottle in clear green glass with a silver mount. Here the masterly simplicity of shape, emphasized rather than disturbed by the flat ornament, reflects endless research into the glass of all periods and countries by Harry J. Powell of London's Whitefriars Glassworks. At a period of intense Continental activity in art glass, Powell held his place among the most distinguished of modern glass artists. *Courtesy of the Victoria and Albert Museum.*

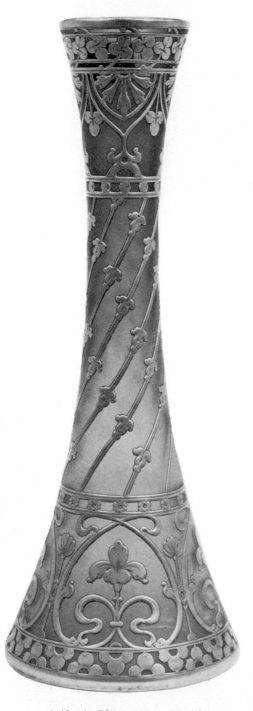

38. (*Below*) Clear ribbed glass perfectly shaped into a stately decanter, made in 1913 by the Whitefriars Glassworks under the supervision of Harry J. Powell. The faint ribbing is repeated in the foot and becomes the dominant feature of the spiralling stopper. *Courtesy of the Victoria and Albert Museum.*

37. (*Above*) Glass vase with silver overlay, the frosted glass shading from purple to clear and the silver in a design of stylized irises, clover leaves and flower heads. Height 13¾ in. About 1900. *Courtesy of Sotheby's Belgravia.*

39. Fruit bowl shaped as swirling leaves and frosted flowers on silver base hallmarked for 1902. Width 11½ in. *Courtesy of Sotheby's Belgravia.*

40. Clear green glass tableware designed by the architect George Walton, 1867–1933, who was associated for a time with Glasgow's C. R. Mackintosh. He moved to London in 1897, designing and decorating houses and designing furniture, metal, cutlery, textiles, carpets and wallpapers. *Courtesy of the Victoria and Albert Museum.*

41. Known as the *SYP* or *Simple Yet Perfect*, an Edwardian Wedgwood teapot reputedly designed by the Earl of Dundonald and here seen in the position for infusing the leaves which are separated from the tea when the pot is righted. The blue pattern is 'Oaklands'. *Collection of Miss Margaret Brentnall.*

42. William de Morgan lustre dish, 14 in. across, painted by Fred Passenger, 1898–1907. *Courtesy of Sotheby's Belgravia.*

43 and 44. (*Above*) Jardinière with a bold pattern of stylized flowers painted in rich majolica glazes, red, blue and yellow, controlled by raised outlines, against a green-printed foliate background. This Minton Secessionist ware was introduced as a popular range in 1902, its name taken from the Viennese Secession movement. Height $7\frac{1}{4}$ in. About 1906. *Private Collection.*

(*Left*) Vase with stylized bird pattern, a favourite with William de Morgan, 1898–1907. *Courtesy of the Victoria and Albert Museum.*

45. (*Left*) Vase, 16¼ in. tall, illustrating one of the fascinating glaze effects developed by Pilkington's Lancastrian Pottery early this century. The firm's chemist, Abraham Lomax, has described how an accidental spilling of a glaze frit resulted in a striated opalescent glaze with veined and feathered effects 'infinitely finer than they could be drawn by a painter', prompting further experiments with some two hundred variants in 1903–4. *Courtesy of the Victoria and Albert Museum.*

46. (*Right*) Covered jar by Bernard Moore dating to the period 1905–15 after he had left the firm of Moore Brothers and experimental work with Doulton chemists to achieve renown with Oriental glazes. Here the decoration is by Hilda Lindop in flambé red on a buff-toned ground. Height 10½ in. *Courtesy of Sotheby's Belgravia.*

47. (*Above*) Sparkling little vase made by self-taught Sir Edmund Elton of Clevedon Court, Somerset, where he worked for nearly forty years, mostly with a single self-taught assistant. Here the simple form is unspoilt by the 'quaintness' of many Elton designs: the metallic glaze, deliberately crackled, probably dates it to the 1900s. *Courtesy of the Victoria and Albert Museum.*

48. (*Right*) Vase by William Moorcroft in Florian ware, the first range of art pottery he introduced for the firm of James Macintyre & Company when he became head of their new art pottery department, about 1898. The vessel has a pleasing surface texture with raised scrolling in the trailed slip that also outlines the stylized flowers, infilled with inky blue on a light blue ground. *Courtesy of Sotheby's Belgravia.*

49. Individualistic vessels from the Della Robbia Pottery, Birkenhead, which in 1905 boasted the approval of G. F. Watts, Holman Hunt, Walter Crane, Alma Tadema and other artists for architectural panels and vases with unique designs and glowing colour. The bowl (*right*) was incised by Charles Collis and painted by James Hughes. *In the Watkin-Garratt collection.*

50. Vase by W. Howson Taylor o[f] the Ruskin Pottery, Smethwick, i[n] production 1898–1935, its shap[e] typically based on early Orienta[l] work to make the most of a rang[e] of brilliant exotic glazes, ever[y] result unique. As early as 1902, th[e] Victoria and Albert Museum pur chased some of Howson Taylor'[s] work, recognizing a quality tha[t] won him international renow[n] throughout the Edwardian perio[d.] Before he died he destroyed hi[s] formulae lest the effects be spoile[d] by commercial exploitation. Thi[s] piece dates to about 1900. *Courte*[sy] *of the Victoria and Albert Museum.*

51. Incised and painted work initialled by artists of the Della Robbia Pottery. *In the Watkin-Garratt collection.*

52. Contrasting styles by leading Edwardian potters William Moorcroft, W. Howson Taylor and F. C. Cope. *Courtesy of the Victoria and Albert Museum.*

53. (*Left*) Teapot by Edward Bingham of Castle Hedingham, the flamboyant design further ornamented with sprigged-on mould-shaped reliefs. *Courtesy of the Victoria and Albert Museum.*

54 and 55. (*Right*) Characteristic Martinware, dated 1903. Probably thrown by Walter and painted by Edwin Martin. (*Below*) Functional tea ware in tin-glazed earthenware from Roger Fry's Omega Workshops, about 1912. *All courtesy of the Victoria and Albert Museum.*

56. Roses as conventional Edwardians loved them, painted on Royal Worcester porcelain. The pair of vases, 8¾ in. tall, painted by Harry Martin, 1910; the boat shape, with bronzed scroll handles and applied lion masks, 1907, from an earlier design by James Hadley and marked with his monogram. *Courtesy of Sotheby's Belgravia.*

57 and 58. (*Left*) Tiny views among gilded scrolling painted by J. H. Plant on a blue Coalport vase, 16¾ in. tall, about 1900. (*Above*) Magnificent studies of swans, favourites with C. H. C. Baldwyn, 1859–1943, a Royal Academy exhibitor, painted on Royal Worcester porcelain, 1907. *All courtesy of Sotheby's Belgravia.*

59. (*Left*) Pierced work signed by George Owen in a Worcester double-walled vase only $3\frac{1}{4}$ in. tall, the outer wall pierced in honeycomb pattern. Three gilt-rimmed quatre-foil openings show landscape sketches in gold and *Mr R. Gray* in script on the ovoid inner body. The delicacy of the work is enhanced by the raised dots of gilded beading and the white 'jewelled' pearling around the shoulder. 1907. *Courtesy of Sotheby's Belgravia.*

60. (*Right*) Pâte-sur-pâte ornament (built up layer-by-layer in thin clay slip and finely tooled before firing) on a slender late Edwardian vase, 11 in. tall, made by Mintons, 1908. The artist, Alboine Birks, has kept within the traditional mythological style customary with such decoration but has introduced an original twist by showing Cupid caught in a shower of rain. *Courtesy of Sotheby's Belgravia.*

Another small group at Woodville concerned mainly with parti-coloured glazes was the Ashby Potters Guild founded 1909 by Pascoe Tunnicliffe of the Victoria Pottery, Woodville. This interesting region is associated, too, with the Edwardians' huge teapots and kettles, some personally named and dated and all splendidly colourful in the uninhibited manner of canal boat painting which has given them the name of barge wares. Typically, the teapot has a miniature pot as its lid finial. Hugh Wakefield has noted that these were made by Tunnicliffe at Woodville from about 1890 to 1910 and also by Mason Cash and Company of Church Gresley and other minor potters of the district.

It was Linthorpe, however, that first won approval for the colours and iridescence of flowing glazes, somewhat similar work being produced until 1904 by the Wilcox firm at Burmantofts Works, Leeds, which employed two of Linthorpe's designers. This other main constituent of Edwardian pottery history, the complicated chemistry of glazes, posed many problems for the artist potter. Harold Rathbone at the Della Robbia Pottery, Birkenhead, for example, frequently introduced incised lines (sgraffito) to control the colours through the firing process. During its brief existence, 1894–1906, this pottery enjoyed the patronage of Victoria, Edward VII and the future George V, but remaining specimens reflect a happy-go-lucky, uncommercialized, studio atmosphere. No two pieces were made alike and frequently they were initialled by both the artist who incised the pattern outlines and the colourist.

Recalling Renaissance work by the Della Robbia family of Florence, Rathbone's aims were to combine the skills of sculptor and potter and to provide a smooth white opaque base for his artists' colours. With the help of an Italian sculptor, Carlo Manzoni, he produced large wall plaques moulded in relief and delicately coloured. These are rare now, however, and the collector is more likely to find the pottery's mark (a medieval ship flanked by the letters DR) on vases and wall plates bearing the period's rhythmic *art nouveau* patterns of flower and leaf. A number of decorators have been identified including Ruth Bare, Charles Collis, James Hughes, H. Jones, Casandia Ann Walker, Liza Wilkins, E. M. Wood and Violet Woodhouse. Their initials and monograms bear out Rathbone's declared purpose to restore 'the individual interest and pleasure in daily work and creation'.

Success with the period's colour glazes was mainly achieved by professionals equipped with the chemistry and furnace technology and the patience—and money—for innumerable experiments. Yet those rich 'Persian' blues, purples and malachite green and shimmering metallic lustres call to mind especially the highly individual and never

E

commercial William de Morgan, 1839–1917. He has been criticized for regarding pottery as no more than a canvas for his two-dimensional ornament. But he developed his own ingenious, unorthodox methods and by Edwardian days was working at Sands End Pottery, Fulham, with the help of Frank Iles and decorators Charles and Fred Passenger, Joe Juster and Jim Hersey. He withdrew for health reasons in about 1907, leaving Halsey Ricardo to continue until 1911. (Frederick Passenger continued the style of Isnik-inspired ornament at the Bushey Heath Pottery, 1923–33.)

De Morgan revelled in capturing, superficially at least, the subtle colours of Near Eastern pottery with its rich, alkaline glazes but his period was rediscovering the coloured and figured glazes of the Far East. The difficulties of kiln control required for such fascinating effects as the flambé or transmutation glazes long absorbed major figures such as Bernard Moore. Around 1901–3 Moore worked with Doulton chemists and the glowing rouge flambé they developed has had long success with the firm at Burslem. In his studio at Stoke, 1905–15, he produced flambé and crystalline glazes, and porcelain as well as earthenware may be found marked with his name and often an artist's monogram. But he had a wider influence as a consultant potter. In 1908 the *Art Journal* observed that 'no ceramic produced in recent years has evoked more enthusiasm than Bernard Moore's peach blow, rouge flambé, gold flambé . . .'

Notable individuals who were important contributors to this fascinating phase of art pottery included W. Howson Taylor, from 1898 at his Ruskin Pottery, Smethwick, and William and Joseph Burton of the Lancastrian Pottery. Howson Taylor, 1876–1935, son of the principal of the Birmingham Margaret Street Art College, won international recognition in the 1900s for his efforts to copy the delicate brilliance of Sung and Ming glazes. His ornaments won awards at the period's international exhibitions and arts and crafts shows. They ranged from tall slender vases to furniture bosses, jewellery and cards of buttons for art-conscious fashion.

From the start he was determined to rely wholly on wheel work for his remarkably thin vessels, 'well potted and without hurry', with no casting or moulding. He decided, too, to use only lead-free formulae for his broken, splashed and flambé glazes in an impressive range of red, brown, purple, light blue and brilliant ruby tones. Other ornament included his soufflé wares in single colours or with mottled effects and some glowing iridescent lustres.

At Pilkington's Lancastrian Pottery ('Royal' from 1913), of Clifton Junction near Manchester, a strong team of artist-decorators brilliantly displayed the fine glazes evolved under the technical and artistic leadership of William and Joseph Burton, with another clever individualist, Gordon Forsyth, as chief designer, and thrower Edward Radford. William Burton, one-time Wedgwood chemist, was a founder member of the Northern Art Workers Guild and a considerable authority on the history of the potter's art. As he told the Royal Society of Arts in 1904, when he first showed his Lancastrian ware in London he was primarily a tile maker, but the development of delicately veined opalescent glazes demanded the rounded surfaces of thrown pottery shapes and made him launch into art pottery in 1903.

The *Art Journal* found suggestions of Chinese, Persian and Greek influence in his forms. Soon here, too, flambé glazes were being produced and brilliant lustres. The intriguing story of glazes, including the flambé effects achieved with a reducing atmosphere in the kiln, is described in *The Royal Lancastrian Pottery 1900–38* by their chemist Abraham Lomax. Ornament was commissioned from leading art designers but some of the most striking came from Forsyth. Under him the small group of artist decorators included Richard Joyce from Bretby, William Mycock who worked at the pottery for 44 years, C. E. Cundall, RA, and Gwladys Rodgers, who did much of the decoration in silver and ruby lustres.

Collectors treasure Forsyth's bold designs in scintillating lustre and can learn much about other glaze techniques from his book on *The Art and Craft of the Potter*. His mark of four scythes in a circle was one of many used by the firm's art staff. The Harris Museum, Preston, displays typical wall plates, relief-moulded to make the most of the mirror-bright lustre.

William Moorcroft, 1872–1945, belongs to this period. In 1897 this trained art teacher started an art pottery venture for the Burslem potters, James Macintyre and Company, where he continued until 1913. In contrast to Moorcroft's own work, this firm is more generally remembered for such endearing notions as imitations of natural stones, registered as agate or tinted porcelain. Their sets of napkin rings, for example, represent six different stones but, alas, tend to break as easily as any other earthenware.

When Moorcroft took control of designs, colours and glazes, he determined that his art wares should be thrown rather than cast, the ornament outlined by hand in the raised lines of slip trailing. His stylized flower forms in soft-toned Florian ware, produced here until 1905, won approval even from the *Magazine of Art* which condemned much garish and inappropriate art pottery. But he is associated especially with the bolder patterns of foliage and fruit, favouring warmer colours against

[57]

inky blue grounds with delightfully luminous glazes that never craze. These were developed about 1910, and the *Art Journal* noticed here, as elsewhere, a new interest in lustres. His firm of W. Moorcroft Limited was launched in 1913, and he was later joined by his son. Minor potters concerned with glaze effects at this time included W. Harrison Cowlishaw of the Iceni Pottery, Letchworth. Some figured lustre glazes by G. L. Ashworth and Bros., successors to the Mason Ironstone firm, are among the collection in Manchester City Art Galleries (maker J. V. Goddard).

Soon this great experimental phase of art pottery was over. But it is the more important to collectors because post-war legislation prohibited the use of free lead and its oxides in glazes, turning the potters to the duller, standard glazes of the wholesaler. By 1913 the *Girls Own Annual* could describe lustre tile painting as a hobby requiring merely the purchase of half-ounce bottles of lustre from Wengers Ltd., and firing by some obliging local kiln or by Lechertier Barbe Ltd. of Jermyn Street, London. Here, too, of course, is a point for the wary collector: amateur pottery decoration was encouraged, with annual exhibitions by such dealers as Howell and James.

Obvious reaction to all this was a return yet again to the English potters' traditional homely wares. Sculptor-turned-potter Reginald Wells, 1877–1951, worked in slip ware and stoneware and made terra-cotta figures from 1904 to 1909 at his Kentish Coldrum pottery near Wrotham and later in Chelsea to 1924, still using Coldrum marks. Roger Fry, 1866–1934, used another early English ware, tin glazed earthenware, white or sometimes blue or green, for plain household vessels in his Omega Workshops, Bloomsbury, from 1913 using the Greek letter as his mark. George Cox produced studio-type earthenware at the Mortlake Pottery around 1910–14 but is remembered mainly for his book *Pottery for Artists, Craftsmen and Teachers*.

Henry Toft, who worked on Mintons' difficult Henri II ware, went later to Wedgwoods and finally had his own pottery making rustic and slip wares until his death in 1909. But the period's restless urge for novelty is most keenly expressed, perhaps, by such potters as William Staite Murray, 1881–1962. This trained artist worked as a potter from 1912, evolving his own style of immensely tall stoneware ornament treated as abstract art, foreshadowing his pupils' surrealism.

*   *   *

It is possible to make fascinating collections from among the Edwardians' many-sided pottery interests, tracing perhaps the change in emphasis from colour to the cool infinities that foreshadow the Leach school. For some collectors there is nostalgia in the major firms' vividly transfer-printed wares or the bewildering range of flower bowls and their pedestals that once thronged winter garden or conservatory. Figures may include statuesque stonewares and terracottas as well as the more obvious drawing-room china styles. But the beginner may well consider a collection of Edwardian tiles. As late as 1906–7 the Debenham house in Addison Road, Kensington, was extensively decorated with fog-defying tiles outside and inside, the architect being William de Morgan's associate Halsey Ricardo. This became renowned as 'the most colourful building in London'.

Tiles offer peculiar pleasures for the ceramics collector, whose collection may perfectly express the atmosphere of an obscure art pottery or even the wild imaginings of an amateur equipped with colours, glazes and tools by the obliging A. F. Wenger. This enthusiasm for wall tiles followed early Victorian rediscovery of encaustic floor tiles, pursued successfully by young Herbert Minton. Many of the firms I have already mentioned included tiles in their manufactures for floors, walls, ceilings, friezes, fireplaces and flower boxes. By Edwardian days most ceramic wall tiles were made by the compression process: dry-as-dust clay was compressed between metal dies, banishing the old worries of warping or cracking in the kiln. Keyed back-shaping ensured a secure hold on the wall. In contrast art pottery tiles moulded in plastic clay—even some of the loveliest De Morgan work—may show ill-fitting corners and uneven surfaces.

Decoration included not only flat hand-painting but colouring over transfer-printed outlines and colour printing by lithography. Colour glazes were applied within the raised outlines known as tube lining, like the old slip trailing, or were separated by incised lines as preferred at the Della Robbia Pottery. Many tiles were shaped in deep relief with press dies to achieve tone contrasts as the colour flowed thickly into the hollows. Some had raised ornaments sprigged-on.

As for subject, these tiles are especially enjoyed today because they cover every aspect of current ornament, far beyond the period's simple geometrical patterns and increasingly formal flower motifs. Where a patterned wall might be over-powering there were many opportunities in frieze and fireplace surround. Hence innumerable figures, from portraits to classical, symbolical and sentimental groups. Many reflect the continuing romantic mood of Wedgwood's Kate Greenaway children, for example, transfer-printed until 1902. Shakespeare, Tennyson, Scott were illustrated and fairy tale characters abounded along with animals by De Morgan and others, reflecting the period's love of nearly-human attributes often formalized into grotesques.

Tiles at that time were still an important part of the home furnisher's wider concern with mural panels of gesso and tempera, ornamented plaster ceilings and the vivid stained glass that in bold outlines and colour intensities had much in common with those panels of small bright six-inch squares. William de Morgan first studied glowing colours in stained glass and became concerned with vase shapes only after gaining valuable experience with tiles. In contrast W. J. Neatby of Doulton's switched, in 1907, from tiles to stained glass.

William Burton had established his position in charge of the technical and artistic sides of the Pilkington tiles works when the firm exhibited one of its earliest successes at the 1901 Glasgow Exhibition, a smooth matt, 'eggshell' glaze, more in keeping with the advanced thought of its period than the glossy surfaces of Victorian work. It was from the great tile making firm of Minton Hollins and Company that Gordon Forsyth entered the Pilkington Lancastrian Pottery in 1906. Tile patterns were commissioned from such leading designers as Crane and Voysey and from Lewis Day who designed for several tile makers although he had long decried the 'hard edge' work still in popular demand.

Doulton's, too, at this period successfully made tiles from many of the wares I have discussed, and contributed importantly to the vogue for architectural panels. These included their majolica ware and rich toned Persian ware (an impasto which suggested painted plaster so that they named it vitreous fresco), and their fog-defying carrara stoneware.

Among Doulton tile patterns there is particular appeal in nursery themes prepared for them by Margaret Thompson whose imaginative work was in demand for tiling hospital wards as far apart as Newcastle and Poona. A charming little art book *Pictures in Pottery*, issued by the firm in 1904, illustrated in full colour the designs for London's University College Hospital, St Thomas's and the Children's Hospital, Paddington Green. Each picture of a nursery rhyme or fairy tale character was composed of some 50 tiles. Correctly the firm claimed that they would prove permanently clean, bright and free from crazing —the tiny cracks frequently caused by atmospheric changes that were deplored by tile critics of the day.

The tile cartoons in the meat hall at Harrods, Knightsbridge, were designed and painted by W. J. Neatby in 1902. Neatby (d. 1910) was at Doulton's until 1907, director of their architectural department. He came from the important Wilcox Burmantofts tile works where a tough local clay was used for tiles modelled in relief for architectural schemes. At this time, however, probably the largest tile making firm was Maw and Company of Broseley, Shropshire, whose tiles are recorded in the Ironbridge Gorge Museum and who received especial praise at this period for 'embossed tiles, sgraffito decorations, slip painting, applied ornament in clay of one colour upon a ground of another, mixed colour glazes . . . '. Flower-enriched wall tiles were particularly well suited to George Maw, 1832–1912, whose interest in Roman tiles prompted study of geology and archaeology and who became an expert, too, on flowering bulbs. His enthusiasm took him frequently abroad, dressing as an Arab in North Africa and being beset by brigands in Asia Minor.

Even Copelands with their overriding interest in tablewares of bone china and fine earthenwares, from Mansion House civic plate to non-chipping hotel ware, produced tiles in great variety. These won the unstinted praise of the potteries chronicler Llewellyn Jewitt, whose skilful designers included R. J. Abraham, 1850–1925. The tiles were moulded from plastic clay, showing characteristic criss-cross combing on the back.

Other tile makers included Sherwin and Cotton of Hanley, associated with portrait tiles using a photographic process; T. A. Simpson and Company of Burslem, not to be confused with the important London tile decorators W. B. Simpson and Sons; J. C. Edwards of Ruabon; W. T. Smith of Longport until 1905; Godwin and Hewitt of Hereford, until 1910; Malkin Edge and Company of Burslem; Richards Tiles of Tunstall from 1903, and the firm of H. & R. Johnson of Tunstall from 1902 which has since combined with many of the Edwardian manufac-turers to become one of the largest ceramic tile companies in the world.

Most flamboyant work in Edwardian days consisted of architectural panels, welcomed by Walter Crane as a relief 'from the doleful gentility of white brick or the depressing grey of stucco'. Typical was the elaborate terracotta Doulton work on Harrods' façades dating from 1902. Already by then, however, this attractive water-impervious material, in its reds, browns and buffs, was becoming somewhat passé, as noted by Julian Barnard in *Victorian Ceramic Tiles*. Now all too few of these large schemes remain—not even the five panels, each 18 ft. by 9 ft., composed mainly of eight-inch tiles, designed and painted by the Pilkington artist Gordon Forsyth, that once lined the staircase leading to Liverpool Museum ceramics gallery. The panels presented anti-quity's contributions to the potter's art, painted in rich colours under alkaline glaze. In these functional days such a theme seems almost as remote as its Babylonian, Persian and Chinese figures. We have to thank those hard-headed, practical tile-makers for the last fairy-tale palaces of romantic fantasy.

Ceramic Marks

Much Edwardian china and earthenware was unmarked, for china dealers preferred to remain the only known sources of further supplies. Nevertheless many marks are to be found, not only among the abundance of art ware decorators but on commercial wares where helpful names and addresses largely replace the early potters' cryptic symbols, apart from a few ever-popular lions, crowns, anchors and galleons.

Comprehensive books are available, such as those by G. A. Godden and J. P. Cushion, to fill in background details even when the clue is no more than an initial or two tucked into the ornamental border around the title of a transfer-printed pattern (which in itself may puzzle the beginner when the title is 'Sèvres', for example, or the ware is 'Whieldon'). Confusion may most easily occur when the tiny letters include the initial of one of the Potteries towns, intended to indicate the firm's address, such as HF for E. Hughes & Co., Fenton or A.P.CO.L. for the Anchor Pottery Co., Longton, though this was more specific than this firm's unlettered foul anchor. Indeed, many a potter recorded the name of the factory rather than the firm, such as Roger Fry's Omega symbol, the 'Tuscan china' marks on wares from the Plants' Tuscan Works, Longton, the church symbols with or without the clue GRESLEY for the Derbyshire firm of T. G. Green & Co., the 'Willow art china' from the Willow Pottery, Longton and the 'Sutherland art ware' made by F. Beardmore & Co., Fenton. Ruskin pottery is now renowned but few collectors, perhaps, would recognize W. Howson Taylor's personal monogram (see below).

When a firm has been identified the collector usually wants to decide the date of his specimen. A few firms helpfully dated their wares in full, such as the Martin brothers on many late ornaments, and Bretby. Copeland's might impress the last two figures of the year, while Pilkington's used Roman numerals for the final figure, from 1905 to 1913. Collectors must not be misled by the inclusion of founding dates in some firms' marks, printed rather than impressed such as Coalport's A.D. 1750.

From 1902 to 1914 Doulton's of Lambeth used an impressed shield with a lower-case letter for the year, from *c* in 1902 to *o* in 1914. Numbers on their Burslem wares may establish the dates when patterns were introduced: D1001 to D4000 covered earthenwares from July 1901 to April 1916; E1 to E9000 the china patterns from October 1901 to January 1914. In a similar way the Registered Number found on many Edwardian wares can establish when a design was first registered as protection from copying but not the exact date of a piece on which it appears. By 1900 these numbers had reached 351202. *England* is almost always included in the mark throughout our period, as required by the McKinley Tariff Act of 1891: the Edwardian trend was to the more specific *Made in England*.

The year symbols used by Minton and Derby are given below. Wedgwood until 1907 used three-letter impressed marks, the third letter signifying the year from *C* for 1900 to *I* for 1906. These letters had been used from 1874 to 1880 but by Edwardian days, as I have already explained, the mark also included the word ENGLAND. From 1907 to 1924 the first letter in the Wedgwood date mark was replaced by a figure 3 but the year-letter sequence continued, with *J* as the final letter in 1907, etc.

At Worcester dates were indicated by dots beside and under the inscription ROYAL WORCESTER ENGLAND around the familiar cursive Ws mark. These dots numbered nine by 1900 and twenty-three by 1914. The numbers relating to shapes of Worcester ornamental wares have been recorded by Henry Sandon: these may be found on the bases of figures, vases, biscuit boxes and the like, from 2101 in 1900 to 2590 at the end of 1914.

After merging with the Worcester Porcelain Company, George Grainger's factory, until 1902, used date letters beneath the word ENGLAND in their mark: these had reached *J* for 1900, *K* for 1901, *L* for 1902.

Often impressed marks are difficult to determine and the collector may look for corroboration among other details in the mark, for most firms introduced many small changes in the wording of name or address, such as the inclusion of *Royal* in the trade mark (Royal Doulton from 1902; Royal Lancastrian from 1913). Often a partnership changed so that the exact wording is important when checking with a marks reference book: as just one example, the 1914 Barum ware change from C. H. BRANNAM/BARUM/N. DEVON to C. H. BRANNAM LTD/BARNSTABLE.

William de Morgan usefully included an address in some marks, only those with the address *Sands End Pottery Fulham S.W.* coming within the Edwardian period. Less immediately recognizable here are marks consisting of initials covering his partnership with the two Passengers and Frank Iles, 1898–1907, such as DIP. Other firms may be elucidated by the trade names concocted from their initials such as LEFICO from the Leeds Fireclay Company and CETEM from C. T. Maling & Sons, Newcastle. Even monograms are not always straightforward, and I illustrate a few of the more obscure, but must leave it to the collector to distinguish, say, the plain JH monogram of Joseph Holdcroft (of another Sutherland Pottery, Longton) from the more familiar James Hadley monogram on Worcester wares.

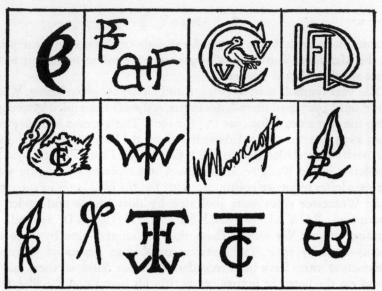

Marks not immediately clear as initials or monograms.
Top row: *Booths Ltd., used on Worcester imitations; two for Burmantofts art pottery faience; personal marks of designers Walter Crane and Lewis Foreman Day, as found on Pilkington wares.*
Centre row: *swan, sometimes impressed, of Charles Ford, Hanley (cf. Minton year symbol); Lovatt & Lovatt, Langley Mill, near Nottingham; William Moorcroft; decorator Louise Powell (for Wedgwood, etc.).*
Bottom row: *decorator Alfred Powell; two marks used by W. Howson Taylor before he introduced Ruskin Pottery into his mark; Torquay Terra Cotta Co.; monogram of Staffordshire decorator Edward Wilkes.*

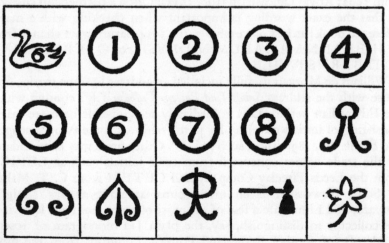

Minton china year symbols. Top row: *1900–1904;* centre row: *1905–1909;* bottom row: *1910–1914.*

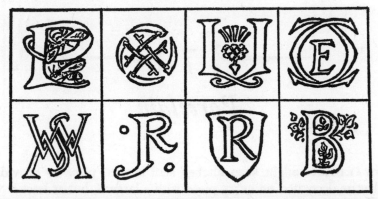

Marks used by Pilkington's Lancastrian Pottery.
Top left: *the firm's mark 1904–1913 (PL with two bees for the Burtons), usually impressed, designed by Lewis Day and replaced in 1913 by the monogram in a Tudor rose. The other seven symbols are the marks of Gordon Forsyth (four scythes); Jessie Jones; C. E. Cundall; W. S. Mycock; R. Joyce; Gwladys Rodgers; Annie Burton.*

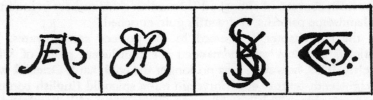

Confusing monograms of Doulton artists: Florence Barlow; Hannah Barlow; Katherine Smallfield; Margaret Thompson.

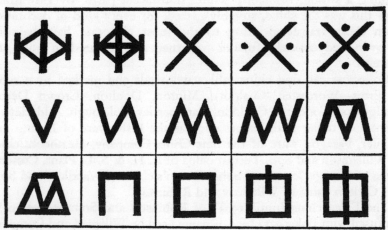

Derby china year symbols.
Top row: *1900–1904;* centre row: *1905–1909;* bottom row: *1910–1914.*

Porcelain

EDWARDIANS might keep kitchen staff in their place by providing tableware decorated on every piece with a large K but at least it was shining white and available in abundance through a period that expected 101 to 105 pieces in a dinner service, 51 pieces for breakfast —even 14 for a double toilet set now collector-cherished if so much as a single basin still has its matching ewer. The king drastically shortened the traditional dinner party, but tablewares continued to be the main concern of almost all Edwardian china makers in innumerable handsome patterns, frequently gold-enriched.

In the last chapter I referred to the potters' earthenwares, but traditional grandeur still demanded the translucent grace of white porcelain. This, however, was no longer the cold, hard, Oriental ware nor eighteenth-century soft porcelain but a splendid English compromise, bone china. This has changed little since Josiah Spode mixed hard porcelain ingredients with nearly half their weight in bone ash, making a strong, brilliantly white, translucent paste. By Edwardian days this was the china, suitably glazed, for every kind of decoration from cheap transfer-printing to the most elaborate hand-painting in oven-fired enamels, further patterned and textured in gold and 'jewels'.

Collectors can find china tablewares made and marked by a score of firms—Worcester, Coalport, Minton, Doulton, Crown Derby, Wedgwood, Copeland, Cauldon, Hammersley, Colclough, Adderley . . . Some sold under trade names such as the Bisto ware of Bishop and Stonier, Paragon ware of the Star China Company, Heathcote china of Williamson and Son, Tuscan china of R. H. & S. L. Plant, Crescent china of George Jones and Sons, Queen's china of Warrilow and Sons and Carlton china of Wiltshaw and Robinson.

The Foley china (until 1903) of Robinson and Sons is not to be confused with Foley art china, a name used by Wileman and Company of the Foley Potteries, whose wares generally sold as Shelley china. Confusingly, too, Silicon china was the name given to an opaque earthenware by Booths of Tunstall making reproductions of eighteenth-century porcelains; Doulton's silicon was a stoneware. Marks of china dealers may be found too, such as Mortlock, Goode, Osler and Apsley Pellatt.

Some of this period's dessert wares are particularly decorative and meticulously finished, and from 1895 Copeland issued charming Christmas plates. But it is especially when these firms looked beyond table-wares that they captured something of Edwardian splendour. For here were ceramics in the grand manner, some prolonging Victorian nostalgia for late eighteenth-century neo-classic elegance, while others strove to reflect the new century's gaiety and grace. Here was wonderful expertise in the handling of colours and gold, yet still the traditionalist's self-assurance to relish highland cattle scenes on huge gilded vases and japonaiseries on 'pilgrim bottles' (no more happily described as 'moonflasks').

The Crown Staffordshire Porcelain Company set about direct reproduction of eighteenth-century glories, from Oriental *famille rose* to Billingsley flower painting. Some other firms did little more than add *England* to their marks on long-loved wares. Belleek for instance (adding *Co. Fermanagh Ireland*) continued some of the delicate parian porcelain that had won them success from the 1860s, such as 'wicker work' vessels built up of fine criss-crossed threads of the paste, serving as a basis for hand-shaped flower encrustations.

This parian ware was another important variety of porcelain. Pioneered by Copeland and Minton in the 1840s, this embellished the home with white figures and ornaments shaped by moulds but with a smooth matt surface suggesting sculpted marble and frequently in professional sculptors' designs. Fine, unglazed, statuary parian was more costly than the glazed parian porcelain used for domestic wares. Collectors do not always realize how widely and how long parian was in production, including, for example, long-favoured Copeland figures. Late pieces might be enriched with colour and gilding but makers may be hard to trace. Even the prolific Robinson and Leadbeater, still concentrating on parian at the end of my period, seldom added their mark.

In addition to unglazed parian figures, the Worcester Royal Porcelain Company used a glazed parian for a creamy-toned ware called stained-ivory, their figures and ornaments including many japonaiseries. This was elaborated in the 'shaded pink' tones achieved by aerograph spraying, and in other colours and brilliant iridescent effects. It was the basis, too, of their subtly glowing bluish-greenish-greyish 'art pottery', Sabrina ware, patented 1894. But this, with its shadowy *art nouveau* decoration, was a far cry from what most Edwardians demanded of Worcester, where extraordinarily expert gilders and painters (views, still life and flowers) continued the traditional Worcester vases, even to a 27-inch Imperial Coronation vase bearing portraits of the new king and queen.

Those of us who were privileged to watch Worcester's grand old man Harry Davis (at work 1898–1969) painting a vase with a Scottish view or a pastoral scene must have a soft spot for this tranquil ornament from another world. Lists of Worcester's Edwardian shapes and details of modellers, painters and gilders are included in the magnificent survey of *Royal Worcester Porcelain from 1862 to the Present Day* by Henry Sandon, enthusiastic curator of the Company's Dyson Perrins Museum.

Worcester collectors need to realize the firm's Edwardian ramifications. By then the interesting James Hadley, long associated with the Royal Porcelain Company, had launched his own factory with his sons, mainly making handsome vases. He died in 1903 but 'Hadley ware' continued long after the firm was taken over by the Company in 1905. Another Worcester factory, Grainger and Company, taken over in 1889, continued in production until 1902 when such important Grainger artists as the highland cattle and game bird painters, John and James Stinton, moved to the main company. Only the firm of Locke and Company remained independent, working in a minor way until it closed in 1904.

London's Franco-British Exhibition in 1908 included Hadley vases and figures, still-life by foreman-painter W. A. Hawkins and 'pierced ivory' work by George Owen. The latter's extraordinarily delicate reticulated patterns had to be pierced through the ware before it was fired, with all the hazards this involved. He continued working until his death in 1917.

The Connoisseur in 1907 condemned the 'average British home' where 'one or two specimens of, say, stereotyped Worcester or of something vaguely Oriental, stand for its occupants' appreciation of ceramic art, endorsed perhaps by a few outrages in majolica of sorts in the dining room'. Certainly the traditional style of decorated vases was upheld, for instance in the very translucent china and transparent glaze of some Cauldon ware (Brown-Westhead Moore and Company until 1904) and at Coalport, a pioneer of leadless glazes, where the Edwardian challenge of threatened depression was met with enlarged premises and a work force of 500.

In the same Sèvres-vase tradition the Minton firm revelled in the work of Continental decorators and especially M. L. Solon, who was renowned for the decoration known as *pâte-sur-pâte*, on vases, plate panels and so on. For this he created a cameo effect on a dark background with a thin cream-like porcelain slip so that the typical mythological scene appeared intensely white in deep reliefs but delicately ethereal where thin. In the *Art Journal*, 1901, Solon described how he brushed on the thin slip, layer after layer, each time-takingly dried, before he could sculpt the reliefs with sharp iron tools; only from experience could he judge how subsequent kiln firing would achieve the 'happy gradation of the transparencies'. When he retired in 1904 he continued decorating plaques (and collecting and writing ceramic books) until he died in 1913.

It is interesting to compare this work with the Victorian 'Limoges' work of Worcester and other factories where cameo effects were suggested by painting upon rich blue grounds in many layers of slightly translucent white enamels; also with the Northwood-Woodall cameos carved at this time in glass (Chapter 5). Solon had several important pupils such as the cousins Alboine, 1861–1941, and Lawrence Birks; his own son Leon was with Mintons until 1909 (and could show his father's delicate touch when portraying, say, a girl playing with a dandelion puff). He was prompted by art school training to experiment widely with *art nouveau*, including 'Secessionist' earthenware (Chapter 6).

This feeling for ethereal grace in cupid's wing and butterfly lingered through my period; indeed the Wedgwood Edwardian bone china lustrewares took on a new brilliance later still, in the post-war fairyland lustre designs of Daisy Makeig-Jones, 1881–1945, who joined the firm in 1912.

Derby in the 1900s won great praise for the delicately finished fruit and flower paintings of Sèvres-trained Desiré Leroy, a naturalized Englishman who worked there from 1890 until his death in 1908. He was particularly successful with white enamel painting on coloured grounds and with flower painting in reserves framed in richly jewelled gilding, being assisted by Darlington (decorator) and Dale (gilder) and followed by Charles Harris.

The company, founded in 1876, had become the Royal Crown Derby Porcelain Company in 1890, and further simplified dating for the collector by including year cyphers. But marks used on eighteenth-century Derby porcelain may be confused with those on Edwardian work (including reissues of many favourite figures) from the town's other porcelain makers, 'the Old Crown Derby China Works'. This was launched by employees of the original Derby factory when it closed in 1848 and continued to use many old moulds and patterns. The traditional Crown Derby mark was continued too, flanked by the letters SH as successive members of the Hancock family participated in the firm until the merger in 1935. Crossed swords replaced the old Derby mark's batons.

Blacker, in the mid-1900s, found much to praise in Royal Crown Derby figures though here again old favourites were reissued, such as Dr Syntax and the Derby Dwarfs. He referred especially to their Persian decoration 'which entirely covers the surface of the piece with intricate designs in colours and gold, raised and sometimes jewelled'.

Gilding was extremely important to all the major china factories. Effects of great richness could be obtained with flat gilding, such as Copeland's renowned 22-carat, 'solid gilt' handles and knobs on the painted ornaments signed by Samuel Alcock, J. Worrall, T. Sadler and others. But through my period several potteries, including Copeland's, introduced gilding in bas relief upon the rims and shoulder surfaces of their most expensive ornamental plates and vases, to gleam softly in the unpolished crevices and shine on the pattern projections.

To achieve such effects the potter-gilder might raise the pattern or recess the background. In either case the surface had to be prepared before the gold was fired on to it. Raised gilding was applied over a pattern in china paste fired on to the surface of the ware. When, instead, the pattern was emphasized by recessing the background this required acid etching to remove those parts of the glaze to a carefully regulated depth, and the process was known as acid gilding.

Yet even this was not always enough, its very grandeur prompting the notion of enriching it with 'jewels'. W. H. Goss, who was Copeland's chief designer before beginning his own business, devised a clever method of securing glass gems by the contraction of the paste in the firing kiln. But Edwardian potters were happy with the technical perfection of gold patterns dotted with finger-pleasing spots of coloured enamels. Borders might be 'white pearled', and plate rims were often closely circled with raised enamel dots of turquoise blue.

W. H. Goss, 1833–1906, had many other claims to attention, such as finger-formed flower jewellery, which Blacker, in the 1900s, noted both in biscuit and in his own mellow variety of ivory porcelain; also traditional painted vases and paper-thin eggshell tea-ware. But in difficult Edwardian days his firm was remarkably successful in using the ivory porcelain for a much humbler style of ornament. This was the armorial china, avidly collected as souvenirs by the growing numbers of tourists and summer holiday makers.

Goss's eldest son, archaeologist Adolphus, was largely responsible for starting this venture, travelling the country to copy exactly to scale the local antiquities he used for many of his models and to ensure correct detail in the armorial work, even on the tiniest half-inch miniatures. All manner of coats of arms were included, not only those of British and foreign royal and titled families and all the obvious towns and counties but colleges, schools, abbeys and so on, hundreds upon hundreds, and many agents were established to ensure appropriate local supplies.

From 1893 tourists with no interest in heraldry were offered souvenir models of famous buildings in natural colours, glazed or unglazed, which in the larger sizes followed the old 'cottage' night-light tradition. Here again Goss's sons were concerned to ensure accurate proportions, whether the subject was the First-and-Last-House at Land's End or Ellen Terry's Kentish farm. Obviously success prompted imitations, and crested china was made in many of the wares I have mentioned earlier, including Carlton, Foley, Tuscan, Willow art china, the Arcadian china of Arkinsall and Sons, and Grafton china of A. B. Jones and Sons, whose 'quaint shapes' in 'transparent ivory china' were sold by Gamages. Crested ivory porcelain made by Glasgow's Nautilus Porcelain Company is interesting, for this firm also made flower-encrusted 'wicker' baskets in the Belleek manner and there may have been some association, as there appears to have been between Belleek and Goss, with movement of craftsmen in both directions.

Today, even on such humble collector-items several books are available, indicating how inferior are many imitations and how great the popular appeal of these beguiling trinkets.

8

Jewellery

MEDIEVAL galleon and frail winged dragonfly, favourite ornamental motifs around 1900, were never more splendid than in the hands of the jeweller. Here assuredly the Edwardian age had begun by the 1890s and lingered on until 1914, as the great jewellery houses shared with individual 'art jewellers' in the brilliant flowering of perhaps the most significant jewellery since the Renaissance.

The basic pieces required of the jeweller change little from age to age. The new century still favoured the mature woman who could flaunt the most magnificent creations. Wildly expensive, status-symbol costume could ensure the requisite swooping figure of around 1901, still lingering on in 1909, with cost-declaring lace and embroidery to soften a silhouette elongated even to its gloves and pointed shoes. But it was the jeweller who had to ensure the perfection of that glittering façade.

Hair was one major problem. Few Edwardians experienced Nestlé's costly permanent wave. For many the desirable swathed coiffure necessitated a toupee or transformation or at least the pads or 'rats' described by V. Sackville-West in *The Edwardians*, 'like last year's birds'-nests, hot and stuffy to the head', concealed under the natural hair. To mask such additions there were jewelled stars and butterflies as well as more spectacular tiaras, still poised on the head rather than shaped to grip it; towards the end of the period, when the hair was spread in wide rolls to the sides of the head, bandeau ornaments were set low on the forehead.

In a period that loved composite jewellery, part of a tiara might be worn as an aigrette to the front or back of the head, sprouting a wispy feather spray; around 1910 it acquired a saucy tilt above the ear. Combs were never more handsome, their gentle tortoiseshell prongs supporting some of the jeweller's most imaginative designs.

Out of doors and at the matinée unwieldy hats required decorative hat pins, especially long and dangerous around 1908–12. Many were sold in pairs and in boxed sets with matching buttons and brooches.

Patents and registered design numbers testify to the pin's importance at this time. Some in boldly asymmetrical *art nouveau* designs bear the makers' initials CH, for the father and son, Charles Horner of Halifax. The son opened a new factory in 1905 where enamelled pendants, too, contributed colourfully to minor *art nouveau* ornaments.

Edwardians took increasing pleasure in ear-rings including the screwed drops and studs required for unpierced ears. But far more important to the gracious swoop of the early Edwardian's swan-like neck was the necklace, especially for evening when bare shoulders could set off magnificent jewels above a froth of chiffon and lace. The necklace was often a flat cobweb collar of fine chains, jewel spangled. But the style particularly associated with the period was the age-masking choker. At its simplest this consisted of thin vertical metal strips threaded with lace or a beaded and buckled ribbon; at its most flamboyant a composition of jewels secured at the back with a tulle bow, or diamond plaques supporting row upon row of pearls. But, like the stiffened blouse collar, the choker necklace was gradually outmoded by the V neckline suggested by the Oriental kimono, newly fashionable around 1910, with all that this implied in a gentler style of evening wear, with floating sash and ostrich feather fan.

A third style of necklace was the long-chain or sautoir falling well below the waist with widely spaced beads—coral, jet, all the simple favourites of the day. While a close-fitting hip line made pockets unthinkable this might usefully carry a watch or pencil. It could be worn throughout the day although Susan, Lady Tweedsmuir, in *The Edwardian Lady* observed that many people associated strings of beads with despised intellectuals along with 'floppy dark green Liberty dresses and flat-heeled shoes'.

Many of the period's new notions appeared in brooches and pendants, the heavy pear shape yielding to the lighter heart outline that was an essential ingredient of this sentimental period along with such romantic emblems of submission as bangles and curb chains, some with padlocks and keys, sold as 'Love Laughs at Locksmiths'. Conventional plaques, bows and sprays were rivalled by the galleon or peacock suggested to the art jeweller by the shape of a piece of opal, perhaps, or a blister pearl. A large, flat pendant might appear to consist of shimmering circles of jewels attracted and held solely by the brilliance of a central, loosely swinging stone. But even by 1910 thin geometrical patterns were accepted. Such firms as J. W. Benson, the Alexander Clark Manufacturing Company and Murlle Bennett and Company, for example, advertised narrow bands shaped as squares and interlaced lozenges in the German-Austrian manner, foreshadowing post-war styles, and thin plaques composed of half-pearls scattered over backgrounds of parallel gold lines.

For evening there were massive composite stomachers such as *The Queen* in 1907 observed on Queen Alexandra: 'her corsage ablaze with crown jewels and long ropes of pearls'.

Special brooches were required for brides and for bridesmaids, for dust-defying motoring cloaks and, of course, for every degree of mourning. Maltese crosses continued, and pendant lockets were popular for tiny photographs. Bow brooches suspended tiny fob watches through a period that approved, also, of watches worn 'on band bracelets, on chains tucked into the front of the bodice and as expanding finger rings' (*The Queen* 1910). There was even a demand for the man's Albert watch chain in woman's size.

Minimal ornament was supplied by the lace pin, like a small bar brooch but with the pin point sheathed lest it catch the flimsy thread. By safety pin brooches the period understood a method of fixing the pin in its hinge, an improvement on simple soldering. In *Life's Enchanted Cup*, the Hon. Mrs C. C. Peel recalled that for tennis 'the meeting place of shirt and skirt was hidden by a petersham belt and kept in place at the back by an ornamental safety pin stuck through the belt'.

Even the late Victorian's ubiquitous bar brooch was in demand with a wider range of inconsequential motifs along the narrow horizontal band of gold, such as Gamages' long popular cross, heart and anchor entitled 'Faith, Hope and Charity'. Some suggested easy flattery: a palette with brushes for the artist, golf clubs for the sportswoman. For the sentimental there was the robin-and-mistletoe or the 'honeymoon' crescent and bee, but like valentines these costume pieces could be absurd or mocking too, with motifs from flies to frogs.

The most interesting sporting pins were quite elaborate tiny creations, in the difficult technique of carved crystal. The dome of translucent crystal was hollowed from behind as a dog's head, insect or the like and the hollow painted in oil colours. A backing of mother-of-pearl or dull bloomed gold gave the motif a three-dimensional effect. These crystals were quite different from the enamels painted by William Essex whose pupil, W. B. Ford, 1832–1922, continued the popular line of tiny dog and horse-head enamels for pins and buttons. J. W. Bailey worked with Ford for a time but his Edwardian enamels are disappointing.

Bracelets, bangles and finger rings, constantly in the wearer's view, were expected especially to express her personal tastes. Flexible bracelets were popular, although cheap chains of flimsy gold might have to be reinforced by hidden metal links. Bangles and rings continued the deep, star-shaped, gipsy setting and coiled snake motifs. The long popular, broad gold band inscribed MIZPAH was a Biblical reference to the place where Laban said to Jacob 'the Lord watch between me and thee, when we are absent one from another'. But rings changed, too, tending to lose the customary widening at the bezel and many acquired a new liveliness in twisted cross-over patterns; late in the period projecting claws in self-effacing platinum gave some an entirely new look.

Being strongly made, frequently of silver, many dressy buckles remain to illustrate Edwardian tastes, happily mocking the sternly simple tailored style worn for cycling, tennis and roller skating or 'rinking'. *The Queen* in 1901 suggested a 'Trianon' straw hat encircled by roses with a black velvet 'Louis XV' bow sparkling with a paste buckle, and late in my period, as skirts shortened a very little, buckles appeared on high-tongued shoes again. Buckles at knee height contributed to the self-mocking absurdity of late Edwardian hobble and peg-top skirts. But by then many of the most handsome, in *art nouveau* designs, were worn by those in revolt against the pencil silhouette, fashionable by about 1908, that was part of the trend towards geometrical abstract pattern.

So much for the period's basic demands upon the jeweller. Even from abroad great jewellers opened branches in Edwardian London where Parisian Chaumet, for example, was already established. Notably Cartier, of the impeccable diamonds and platinum, opened in London in 1902. In 1903 Peter Carl Fabergé, 1846–1920, a Russian of French Huguenot descent, offered London the lovely materials and techniques of his St Petersburg workmasters. All revelled in a welcome so warm that jewellery was never more exciting, but so brief that already collectors are concerned with its recognition and rescue.

The leading Edwardian jewellery firms remain familiar names—Asprey, Collingwood, Garrard, Hennell, Kutchinsky, Wartski and the rest, required by the sheer cost of their materials to maintain high standards of craftsmanship little affected by the industrial revolution. Yet while tradition dominated the designs requested by the affluent it is possible to trace a pattern of change through Edwardian years. Here the unique Hennell stock books are of inestimable value, offering page after page of coloured drawings exactly dated from 1887 onwards, by A. W. Tutt. At their best these firms all achieved Peter Hinks' definition of 'Edwardian'—gaiety, fantasy and elegance, tempered with dignity and precision.

For the great commercial firms this was the period of the precious stone. Diamonds especially were immensely admired for size and quality. Roger Fry in the *Burlington Magazine*, 1910, dismissed this concern for 'nothing but the market value' but those splendid gems, sensitively presented, wonderfully reflected Edwardian Baroque grandeur.

New South African mines had been developed from the 1860s, and by 1910 diamond cutting and polishing had been reintroduced in England, including a new process of sawing. More perfect cutting ensured maximum splendour as light was reflected forward again from within the stone. The familiar 58-facet brilliant cut was rivalled by the pointed oval marquise and the triangular-faceted briolette drop, before the 1930s welcomed the coldly rectangular baguette and emerald cuts.

There was more to this spectacular Edwardian glitter, however. White settings for diamonds had always been of silver, gold backed lest they smudge delicate skin or fabric. But 'white gold' could be achieved by including nickel as a kind of bleach in the alloy and this again was a process developed in Edwardian days. By 1913 the Birmingham firm of E. Day was making 15 carat white gold. Soon palladium might be used instead of the nickel—costlier but more easily worked.

At this time, unlike gold, platinum still lacked the prestige of hall marks. But it was in Edwardian days that jewellers gradually exploited its immense potential—clean, white, requiring great heat for working but so strong that settings could be cobweb light, the stones often gripped merely by delicate claws that allowed the light all around in the setting known as *à jour*. Saw-pierced platinum offered a delicacy suggesting lace, perfectly suiting the sense of light and movement the period loved; self-explanatory 'knife wires' appeared from the front to be even thinner than they really could possibly be. The firm of Mappin and Webb in 1904–5 declared boldly that 'no more metal is left than is necessary for the safety of the settings. The effect and beauty is derived from the gems'.

Subsidiary stones in increasing demand included opals, partly met by the development of the fabulous Lightning Ridge black opal field in New South Wales in 1905, followed by discoveries in Queensland. Fire opals, water opals, all possess the wonderful flashes of vivid colour at their heart but tempted the lapidary to cement thin wisps into 'doublets' or 'triplets'.

Other period choices included increasingly available turquoise, 'lucky' moonstones, zircon heated to a cold blue tone, topaz, alexandrite (green by day and red by artificial light) and Edward VII's favourite light green peridot. Another favourite, now comparatively rare, was the demantoid garnet, beautifully lustrous with flashes of gold in colours from emerald to the yellowish-green of chrysolite. Peter Hinks warns collectors to look for its golden filaments of asbestos, never seen in the cheaper peridot.

Green is assuredly one of the period's colours, and the blue that could be captured brilliantly, too, in enamels, sometimes with touches of yellow and fiery red. Always available, too, was jet and the 'French jet' that was merely cold, black glass.

At the end of the period a Japanese perfected the cultured pearl—and Edwardians of course liked pearls with everything, from the duchess's eleven-row choker to her maidservant's lucky wishbone brooch. The latter market happily accepted the compromise of the gold-mounted half pearl, for innumerable Edwardians were delighted with the cost-cutting Midlands jewellery industry, home of brilliant mass production methods such as the stamping of mounts and clever chain work.

All the leading stores could offer pendants, brooches and bangles for shillings rather than pounds. Even the most heavily alloyed 9-carat gold was improved from around 1900, from an unpopular coppery tone to a warm yellow, and synthetic jewels were brilliant imitations of the real thing. The Parisian Diamond Company, for example, with three London West End addresses, took pride in close imitations. The *Lady's Pictorial* declared that a string of their pearls might be worn beside 'a row that costs 3000 sterling and the clearest north light will disclose no inequalities of value'.

Such were the possibilities of Edwardian jewellery. Today's collector differentiates between the jewellery that met the general commercial demand with lighter, more fluid versions of traditional classical design, and more extreme expressions of a tossing, swinging *joie de vivre*.

Looking for influences, the collector is confronted by the contrasting moods of the art jewellery leaders supported by prolific local art schools. Here the results are often so pleasing to modern eyes that it is easy to over-estimate their importance among contemporaries. Indeed some authorities, such as Ernle Bradford, have argued that the art jewellers' attenuated figures, twisting leaves and 'Beardsley' scrollwork are little better than the mechanical classicism of many commercial firms.

As in their silversmithing, the revolt they sought to express was two-fold—against machine-dominated commercialism and against traditional academic classic ornament. The one prompted their romantic medievalism and the scrupulous workmanship associated with the arts and crafts movement, the other the evanescent ornament of *art nouveau*. In theory these were poles apart, yet even those who protested most loudly were deeply influenced by this determined disassociation with the past—such as Sir Alfred Gilbert, R.A., for example. This marvellously imaginative sculptor-designer transformed the image of official regalia by designs incorporating the whiplash curves and even the lyrical figures that were at the heart of the new cult.

In many parts of the country towards 1900 eager vocal groups of jewellery designers and craftsmen were enjoying personal craftsmanship individually or shared within their romanticized conceptions of medieval guilds. Even as late as 1910 *The Studio*'s first prize for a gold bracelet was won by 'Sir Esperance', showing four romantic-medieval scenes linked by flying arrows. Instead of gold and platinum these men and women favoured silver, hand beaten, carved, engraved, inlaid, enamelled, with a surface polished only to a softly glowing lustre. Aymer Vallance of *The Studio* found cause for praise in the fact that a silver clasp designed by Oliver Baker showed strapwork that 'looks as though it might have been produced by casting from a model but as a matter of fact is entirely wrought and folded by hand'.

Instead of the wealth-proclaiming sparkle of huge faceted diamonds, they favoured moonstone, colour-changing opal, amethyst, chrysoprase and the challengingly irregular baroque pearl, with obvious disregard for their relative values and all intermingled with the colour and texture-subtleties of enamels. Henry Wilson, for example, in his popular book on silverwork and jewellery, 1902, 1912, declared that 'the glitter takes away that mysterious magical quality, that inner lustre of liquid light . . . the stones rejected by the jeweller are almost always well worth the attention of the artist.'

Henry Wilson, 1864–1934, was typical of his period in training first as an architect before establishing himself as jeweller and metal worker, teacher at the Royal College of Arts and L.C.C. Central School and an immensely important figure in the arts and crafts movement. His apprentices included George E. Stedding, who set up his own London workshop in 1907, and H. G. Murphy, 1884–1939, who in turn taught at the Royal College of Arts and became principal of the Central School of Arts and Crafts. It is interesting to trace Wilson's direct influence, too, upon a fellow architect-turned-silversmith, John Paul Cooper, 1869–1933 (Chapter 3). Bernard Instone worked for a time in Cooper's studio at Westerham, Kent.

In Chapter 3 I have referred to C. R. Ashbee and his Guild and School of Handicraft. In his book *Craftsmanship in Competitive Industry*, 1908, he claimed that he had had jewellery designs stolen and reproduced more cheaply by using machines and bad working conditions.

In a gold pendant that cost him £2 18s 9d to produce (selling at £4 7s 6d), the labour and workshop costs came to £1 11s 8d—considerably more than the gold (11s 4d) and stones (12s 7d). His designs show the craftsman's imagination exploiting the natural shapes of his stones in some of the period's favourite motifs. But it must be admitted that, for all their gentle silverwork and delicate wires, many of his designs were ill-tuned to the frothy, frivolous dress favoured by most of those who could afford his prices.

In the same mood, Nelson Dawson, 1859–1942, one of the founders of the Artificers Guild, studied enamelling under the noteworthy Alexander Fisher. But it was his wife Edith who did most of the work for their successful partnership. Indeed women played a considerable part in this great outburst of jewellery. Ernestine Evans Mills, for example, was a clever Fisher pupil, at work for half a century. Even William Morris's daughter May, 1862–1938, designed jewellery as well as her more familiar embroideries and founded the Women's Guild of Arts.

Sadly, enamels quickly lost favour although some exquisite work was achieved in the most difficult *plique-à-jour* process of unbacked cloisonné enamel for dragonfly wings and the like. Perhaps Giuliano from Naples had set too high a standard for enamelled jewellery in Renaissance style when he settled in late Victorian London.

In Birmingham, Arthur and Georgie Gaskin were staunch supporters of the arts and crafts movement. Here again husband and wife worked together. A drawing book of Gaskin designs from 1902 to 1923 was on view at the Birmingham gold and silver 1773–1973 exhibition. This showed the change from early symmetrical patterns of wire around a central jewel to increasing complexities, with considerable use of enamel from 1906 and tiny silver birds from about 1910. W. T. Blackband, 1885–1949, was a Gaskin pupil who executed some of their designs and continued the style well into post-war years; he achieved great delicacy in handling gold by an ancient granulation technique.

The collector aware of this strong undercurrent of sound, painstaking craftsmanship can understand why English art jewellers seldom became wildly involved with the fantasies of *art nouveau*, expressed, for example, by the renowned Parisian René Lalique, 1860–1945, who eventually lost his heart to the endless possibilities of glass. In 1903 and 1905 his work was displayed in London, already familiar to him from two years of study in his youth. In Belgium, Philippe Wolfers, 1858–1929, had the backing of the huge firm of Wolfers Frères for his sometimes heavy *art nouveau* jewellery in African ivory and other unusual materials. Graham Hughes has drawn attention to the fact

Pelleas et Mélisande—*typically delicate romantic pen drawing by the designer Jessie M. King. Reproduced in* The Studio, Winter number *1900–1, for which it was specially drawn.*

that from 1893 to 1908 Wolfers' designs became known all over the world through appearing in 83 magazines including *The Studio, Artist,* and *Magazine of Art*.

In England, many jewellers enjoyed contrasting formal pattern with upthrusting plant stems and whiplash curves in softly coloured leaf and petal. The early 1900s with their love of exotic symbolism and mysterious, unworldly beauty welcomed Celtic design and elusive abstractions suggesting enigmatic women's faces with the essential sense of movement expressed in their wind-tossed hair. Inevitably even these were commercialized, stamped in low relief on Edwardian silver brooches and buttons.

At their dreamiest the faces are associated especially with the jewellery of the Glasgow school including Herbert MacNair, with his weird, half-suggested shapes, and the Macdonald sisters (See Chapter 2). Talwin Morris, 1865–1911, another architect in the group, experimented with beaten aluminium for buckles and clasps, its lightness permitting substantial-looking formal shapes. These suited the group's mid-Edwardian change of mood to angular patterns such as superimposed rectangles. In the same group Jessie M. King, 1870–1949, occasionally designed silver jewellery for Liberty, her conventionalized flower groups broadly composed, with little fine detail. She was a tireless worker but probably happier among the star-decked maidens and anguished knights of her book illustrations and other craft work.

Not surprisingly the period's women jewellers have left many imaginative buckle designs, their ornament spanning the general change of emphasis from whiplash curves to rectilinear abstractions. Arthur Lazenby Liberty found two-part clasps particularly successful when he launched his Cymric gold and silver work (Chapter 3). This presents the collector with many problems and pleasures. No individual designers were named and it was left to contemporaneous critics to identify such contributors as Oliver Baker and Bernard Cuzner, whose designs are by no means confined to the *art nouveau* characteristics associated with Edwardian Liberty's.

The firm is important as being one of the few to make a notable commercial success of art jewellery notions in London and the provinces, among customers unlikely to question the use of large-scale factory processes that permitted competitive prices. Brooches and pendants might be fashioned in attractive interlacings of silver wire, touched with coloured enamels. When the central gem was a softly iridescent moonstone a pendant could sell for as little as 14s 6d. Even the mounting of stones on such items as silver clasps (typically die-stamped rather than hand wrought) was accomplished cheaply and

[81]

harmoniously when they were pressed from the back through holes cut in the face of the softly glowing silver without fussy collets. (The studio art jeweller would be more likely to *pavé*-set the jewel in a hollow scorpered out of solid metal.) A necklet of moonstone and amethysts set in gold was priced at £4 10s in the *Lady's Pictorial* in 1910. So perfectly did this subtly gleaming stone meet the aesthetes' pleasure that the firm publicized it in a special brochure. Collectors may note that the Birmingham firm of W. H. Haseler, who executed Liberty designs, also supplied other London establishments, possibly including Murlle Bennett and Company who sold jewellery in the sensitive *art nouveau* manner as well as cold German formalities.

Many lesser known firms and individuals made art jewellery too, using silver, enamels, niello and minor jewels for their galleons and dolphins, their dragonflies and dreamy women, among them Annie McLeish, Kate Fisher, Kate Allen, Winifred Hodgkinson, Edgar Simpson. David Veazey devised enamelled patterns elusive as smoke. But the phase soon passed. Many whose work was applauded in 1902 were forgotten by 1909, their enthusiasms outmoded by the forceful shapes that went with bright colours, bizarre costume and hectic dance movements in the first years of George V's reign.

9

Costume Accessories

SADLY, Edwardians witnessed the fan's retreat. But at least it gave a magnificent valedictory display. Never was it grander or more decorative, with glittering leaf or curling plumes and bold sticks hung with ribbons, tassels or loops of seed pearls. It is easy to find reasons for the gradual decline. The costly theatrical glamour of the 1900s' larger-than-life fashion fantasies could never last. As Richard Ormond has pointed out, even the fashionable portrait artist John Singer Sargent found them unpaintable (as did Augustus John) but how he enjoyed the period's fans, wide spread in their vast glory.

With one hand required to control the heavily pinned hat tearing at her high-piled hair and one to drape her sweeping skirts, it is hard to imagine how any woman contrived to handle her bag, parasol and feather boa, let alone a fan. Yet fashion comment in 1903 described a fan as 'just what one wants for matinee or outdoor use'. For what G. Woolliscroft Rhead described as the period's 'romping dances' the fan might hang from the waist on a chain and clip 'fan suspender'.

Fan styles that may be attributed to my period include the frankly nostalgic beauties harking back to the fan's eighteenth-century heyday; the dressmaker styles reflecting current costume; and wholly new ideas attempting to involve fans in intriguing, personal themes.

Queen Alexandra, Queen Mary and Queen Mary's mother, the Duchess of Teck, all dearly loved the fans they carried on important occasions. An Edwardian fan, 13½ inches long, typical of Queen Mary's taste for traditional splendour and given to one of her dressers, had a leaf painted with butterflies and putti pulling a carriage through a night sky starred with real diamonds. This was the nostalgic style, attempting to recapture the fantasies of France under Louis XV and Louis XVI, with romantic fancy dress figures in landscapes among beribboned trophies. Elaborations of rococo scrolls patterned the sticks supporting the leaf and the stronger end-guards that might be of painted ivory or gilded mother-of-pearl. A fan sold at Christies in this manner could be dated exactly by its inscription 'Dublin Castle March 4th 1903'.

A quite different kind of nostalgic fantasy associated fans with a Kate Greenaway world of subtler charm and dreamy colouring. T. Houghton signed a few of these. Charles Conder, c.1868–1906, was remembered and copied throughout Edwardian days for figure scenes costumed vaguely in the past yet expressed in the patterns and misty pastel colours of his day. More remarkably, occasional fans of this period came from quite a number of easel-and-canvas artists, stemming from wide acceptance of once-despised Japanese art, throughout a period when Japan was exporting fans by the million.

Often, like the Japanese themselves, these artists appear to have been thinking of ornament to be viewed flat rather than in folding fans. Some tried too ambitiously to introduce architectural backgrounds ruined by the fan's fold lines. Others, such as George Sheringham, thronged the leaf with tiny figures as closely grouped as in the familiar Mandarin fan but hopelessly confused since they lacked the Oriental glitter and the hard outlines of those strange little appliquéd faces.

Frank Brangwyn, A.R.A., Charles Shannon, A.R.A., and H. Granville Fell, among others, produced occasional fan designs. So did a number of women artists including Mrs George Gascoyne, Ethel Larcombe, Muriel Baker, Jessie Bayes, Joan Joshua and Elizabeth Yeats. The ubiquitous designer Jessie M. King was represented by Woolliscroft Rhead in the Art Journal, 1911, by The Dance of the Autumn Leaves. Like most of these artists' fans this is just a wispy painting on vellum of figures among trees. Christine Angus's work may be dated by her introduction of lettering around the leaf in the period's characteristic script (see Chapter 10). But sadly the result of all this artist participation was confusion in design rather than the revival hoped for by Woolliscroft Rhead whose huge 1910 book on fans is now a rare and much quoted classic.

Nevertheless there is much to enjoy in the period's strivings towards more graceful artistic expression. Dreamy, elongated figures in curving postures of art nouveau might be almost lost among writhing wispy foliage, but in delightful colour schemes from Queen Mary's favourite delphinium blues to tawny autumn tints. Flowers, too, were never painted more charmingly nor the period's adored dragonflies.

Fans with hand-painted leaves of paper or parchment required an opaque ground such as gouache or Chinese white but could sell for a few shillings, whereas more costly, pliant kid, known as chicken skin, could take the artist's ethereal transparent colour. But most artists compromised with silk taffeta. Woolliscroft Rhead suggested etched fans might well be revived, and produced designs ranging from a costumed wedding scene to a dreamy mermaid fantasy. A few practical fan decorators such as Reginald Dick and Thomas Cook speeded their work with stencils, recognized by a repetition of detail suggesting wallpaper. In 1902 a typical hand-painted fan of gauze-mounted silk on sticks of gilded horn suggesting tortoiseshell might sell for 45s. London makers and wholesalers throughout Edwardian days still listed painted, gauze, lace, satin and feather fans as well as the 'paper fans for advertisements' more generally associated with post-war years.

Size of leaf is little guide to date among Edwardian fans. The 1900s continued the 1890s' huge half-circle—sometimes beyond the half-circle—usually with 14 to 16 sticks as well as the end guards and measuring 13 inches or more from rivet to border. But there was a revival, too, of tiny Empire fans with six or eight sticks as part of the high-waisted early nineteenth-century look. Among these revivals, and 'ultra fashionable' in 1903, was the small 14-stick fan more roundly shaped than usual; trick fans included the telescopic device drawn into a circle by pulling cords through a hollow handle of olive wood.

More appealing was a continuing pleasure in the sequins that had been in and out of fashion ever since the late eighteenth century had hammered them into brilliance from tiny loops of wire. Those on Edwardian fans were stamped or punched from thin metal sheets in many shapes and colours. They were generally approved by fashion commentators because they could be 'relied on not to "show date" '. In a good quality fan the sequins lightly stitched to the leaf were matched by tiny metal discs fixed to guards and sticks in the manner of *piqué clouté*.

Often spangles shimmered on fans of lace. Never was lace more appreciated than by rich Edwardians who could recognize at a glance when the Brussels mount was rendered even more desirable by insertions of *point de gaze*. In 1903, Youghal convent lace makers presented Queen Alexandra with a lace fan that declared in Celtic 'I cool, I refresh and I can keep secrets'.

Typically *The Connoisseur* in 1905 carried a fan advertisement offering to supply 'replicas of old designs from customers' own lace'. Mappin and Webb in 1910 offered 9½ inch fans of duchess lace with panels of point lace on mother-of-pearl or blonde tortoiseshell sticks priced from £3 15s to £6 10s. Sometimes the lace was applied to a basis of net—black lace on white for example, 'lightly sewn with minute silver spangles, the sticks carved and pierced bone', priced at 9s 6d in 1902. By late Edwardian days the bolder colour combination might be gold net over purple silk. Sometimes the lace was uneasily augmented with painting. A presentation fan to the wife of the Fanmakers' Company Master in 1900 even combined traditional lace with a painting of City of London Imperial Volunteers en route for South Africa.

Sticks of a lace fan may be perforated ivory but a particularly attractive foil is plain-cut mother-of-pearl. The vivid lustre gleams in rainbow colours through the lace to the tips of the sticks in the finest work though this might necessitate two invisible joins in every stick of a 13 inch fan. In cheaper work only the brins—the lower, visible part of the sticks—prove to be of pearly shell, often in a slightly waved outline, or of ivory or cheaper imitative bone. Other sticks and guards were made of tortoiseshell, imitated in horn, and of the cheap, tawny-coloured favourite known as imitation amber.

Experimental arts and crafts work included guards of silver filigree and enamel, and more were of wood offering attractive ground for gilded or silvered ornament. F. Vigers was known to Edwardians for his guards and sticks of carved sandalwood. Some were sold plain for the amateur to decorate with paper scraps or enamel colours. There was even a vogue, lingering from the 1890s, for plain autograph fans, often of fragrant cedar or sandalwood. The *brisé* design was especially suitable, with the strong ribbon-linked sticks widened to overlap and needing no leaf. The surfaces of ivory or wood were suitably prepared for celebrities to inscribe their names and whims of fancy.

Just as some of Europe's earliest fans were elegant tufts of feathers so feather fans were the last on the scene. These included bold peacock tail sprays, exquisite little fans of swansdown and meagre creations of long-pillaged osprey. A charmingly simple *brisé* fan might be composed of eight or more pure white swan feathers; sometimes around 1900 the feather shapes were cut in stiffened silk and merely edged with down to soften the outline. Perhaps the most extraordinary, sad little feather fan was made in 1900–01. This was composed of tiny shaded feathers, one from each wing of 3260 woodcock shot by the Duke of York and his friends. It took a woman over a year to stitch them to the fan's 20 sticks of red tortoiseshell.

Ostrich feathers were made into the largest fans, perhaps 30 inches long, wonderful to handle. Skilled preparation made the plumes curl inward at the tips. Sticks were usually of tortoiseshell to minimise weight, blonde tortoiseshell being the most costly. Here especially was a chance to express the excitement of colour disharmonies appropriate to the hectic, late Edwardian scene. All the pink-to-orange-to-flame tones appeared at their most sensuously splendid in widespread

61 and 62. Figures by the Worcester Royal Porcelain Company. *The Violinist* was introduced in the 1890s and remained popular through Edwardian days. The finish is 'stained ivory', given extra clarity with gold to outline the costume detail. Height 9¾ in.

The Volunteer in Khaki was one of six Boer War soldier figures modelled in 1900. The dry colouring is in shades of brown with details in gold. Height 7⅝ in. *Both courtesy of the Dyson Perrins Museum, Worcester.*

63 and 64. (*Right and below*)
Two examples of pierced
ornament in Worcester
porcelain. The three-footed
pot pourri bowl, 8 in. wide,
was made in 1909, the osprey-
supported vase, 8⅝ in. tall,
in 1913. *Both courtesy of
Sotheby's Belgravia.*

65. (*Right*) Miniature covered vase,
5¾ in. tall, in 'jewelled' Royal
Crown Derby porcelain, the exotic
bird painted by Sèvres-trained
Desiré Leroy, who worked for
Derby 1890–1908. *Courtesy of
Sotheby's Belgravia.*

66. Ornate japan pattern in Imari style on items from a Royal Crown Derby tea service. Colouring is the familiar rich mazarin blue, iron-red and green, shimmering with pencil gilding, 1912–16. *Courtesy of Sotheby's Belgravia.*

67. Goss cottages, 2¾ to 4 in. wide. Upper row: (*left and right*) David Lloyd George's home, grey roofs, creeper-covered walls, one showing the addition of an annexe; (*centre*) Huer's House, Newquay, Cornwall, unglazed, mainly pale grey. Lower row: (*left to right*) First-and-last House in England, without annexe; Old Maids Cottage, Lee, Devon and Manx cottage, both with thatched roofs and creepers. *Courtesy of Sotheby's Belgravia.*

68 to 71. Exquisite illustrations from the exactly-dated pages of design books kept by R. G. Hennell & Sons. *Above*: brooch designs dated 1906, in sapphire, diamond and pearl, and in ruby, diamond and pearl. *Left* and *below*: pendants, the diamond heart-shape dated 1909, the quatrefoil in diamonds and platinum, 1899–1908. *Courtesy of Messrs Hennell Ltd.*

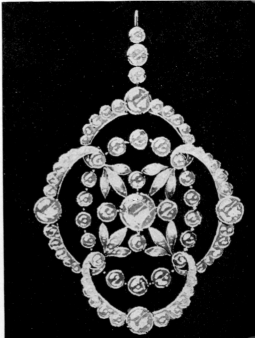

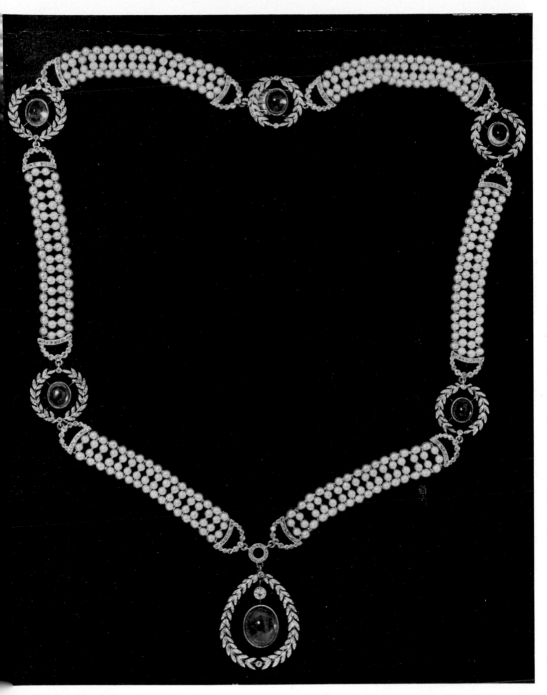

72. Row upon row of pearls served elegant Edwardians in innumerable neck-concealing chokers, but by 1910 the fashion was passing. Here Oriental pearls in similar abundance have been mounted as a collar necklace, the links and pendant formed of cabochon-cut sapphires linked to encircling laurel wreaths of diamonds by almost invisible platinum. About 1910. *Courtesy of Messrs Harvey & Gore.*

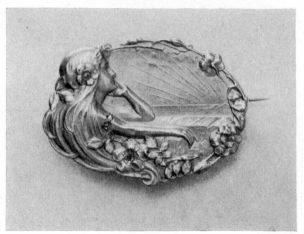

73. (*Left*) Small gold brooch, 1½ in. wide, set with rose diamonds, the design typical of the 1900s mood, with the dreamy maiden gazing from ramparts towards a sunrise beyond the sea. *Courtesy of Sotheby's Belgravia.*

74 and 75. (*Above and right*) Other motifs equally popular with the art jeweller. The sparkling dragonfly has articulated wings in plique-à-jour enamel and is diamond-trimmed on head, body and wings, to be worn as brooch or hair ornament. *Courtesy of Christie's.*

The peacock pendant was designed by C. R. Ashbee and made by his Guild of Handicraft, 1903. *Courtesy of the Victoria and Albert Museum.*

76. The flat style, that was an important feature of the period's more conventional jewellery, illustrated in designs ranging from butterflies and bows to geometrical patterns, well suited to the meticulous workmanship required for diamonds and platinum. *Courtesy of Messrs Harvey & Gore.*

77. (*Left*) Widely different styles of ornament, but all glass scent bottles. (*Left to right*): green glass with silver overlay, hallmarked Birmingham 1901; opaque white and pink; ruby glass enamelled with lily of the valley within heart-shaped gilt scrolling. *Courtesy of Sotheby's Belgravia.*

78. (*Right*) The 7½-in. fan has a mount of shimmering gauze, its border of painted silk edged with spangles. The 'period piece' beside it is an eye-shade, held like a lorg-nette. When not in use, the shade (with embroidered pansy ornament) is secured against the handle; when released it opens to a con-venient slant. *In the Mary Ireland collection.*

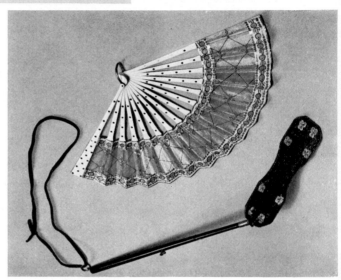

79. Glass scent bottles in double-ended or union design to contain both scent and smelling salts. *Left*: deeply mould-shaped for heat resistance, sold by Mordan & Company. *Centre*: flashed glass, from Maw & Son. *Right*: here the bottle's central division can be seen through the blue-patterned clear glass. The open hinged lids show the inner glass stoppers. *Courtesy of the Harris Museum and Art Gallery (Mrs French collection), Preston.*

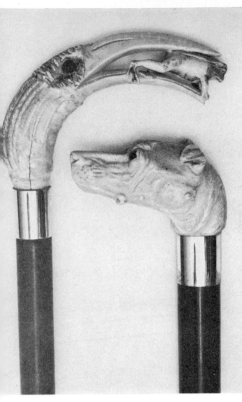

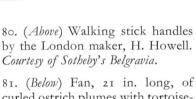

80. (*Above*) Walking stick handles by the London maker, H. Howell. *Courtesy of Sotheby's Belgravia.*

81. (*Below*) Fan, 21 in. long, of curled ostrich plumes with tortoise-shell guards and brins. The colour ranges from pale blue at the tips through neutral to soft apricot. *In the Mary Ireland collection.*

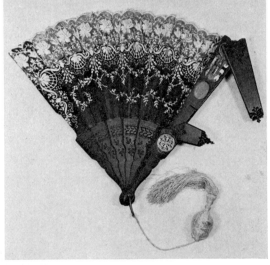

82 and 83. (*Above*) Two Thornhill 'dressing case' fans. The mask fan has silver pencil, scissors and button-hook slotted into the guard's silver ornament. The lower fan has one guard opened to reveal scissors, needlecase, etc. Its other guard hides comb and manicure tool and there is a thimble in the tassel bob. *In the collection of Mrs Bertha de Vere Green.*

84. Satin screen panel in brilliantly coloured silks and silver-gilt thread, worked at the turn of the century by Miss E. D. B. Bradby, 1861–1927. *Courtesy of the Victoria and Albert Museum.*

85. Edwardian handkerchief in muslin embroidery even more exquisite than its edging of lace. The double-heart motifs suggest that this is a betrothal gift. About 12 in. square. *In the Mary Ireland collection.*

86. Delicate specimen motifs made by the Diss Lace Association, Norfolk, launched in 1902 as a self-supporting cottage industry by the enthusiastic teacher-organizer, Miss Alice Savory.

87. Fan of white Honiton lace containing two gauze insertions painted in pale yellow and white (mimosa and may blossom.) The guards and brins are of colourful mother-of-pearl and the upper sections of the sticks are pierced to appear inconspicuous behind the lace. Length 13¾ in. *In the Mary Ireland collection.*

POMONA

88. *Pomona* in rich William Morris style of surface-covering embroidery. The subject was taken from a Morris tapestry woven in 1896 with the figure designed by Burne-Jones and a background adapted by J. H. Dearle. A companion panel, *Flora*, is in similar style but with lilies in the foreground and a border of clematis and passion flowers.

89. Cushion cover of about 1900 decorated with coloured silks and linen appliqué by Jessie Newbery, teacher of needlework at Glasgow School of Art. Glasgow's notable new style of embroidery was welcomed by the *Studio*, 1910, because 'it takes the everyday things of life and . . . seeks to make them beautiful as well as useful'. *Courtesy of the Victoria and Albert Museum.*

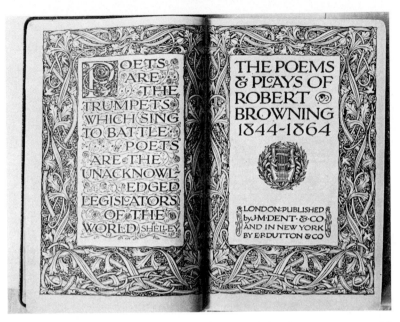

90. Title page of a book published in 1906 in the very successful *Everyman* series. This offered the 'thousand best books' in an inexpensive but graceful format, showing considerable William Morris influence in the foliated borders and the lay-out of the lettering. *In the collection of Miss Alison Kelly.*

91. Title page of an edition of Shakespeare published in 1908. The laurel motif, suggested by the poet's crown, has been combined with fluttering ribbons and elaborate italic lettering to produce an effect of Edwardian rococo. *In the collection of Miss Alison Kelly.*

92 and 93. (*Left and below*)
Greetings postcards of about
1905. The valentine card
made of violets spangled in
purple; the Christmas travellers, signed *F. Bianco*, issued
by Raphael Tuck, perhaps
for the American market.
Both private collection.

94 and 95. (*Below*) Christmas
greetings postcard in Raphael
Tuck's 'Oilette' series. Postmarked 1905.

Below right. Postcard published by S. Oates &
Company, Halifax, with
permission from W. H. Goss.
The characteristic piece of
Goss heraldic china, bearing
the Burnley arms, was claimed
to be based on a Roman ewer
found at York. Postmarked
1907. *Both private collection.*

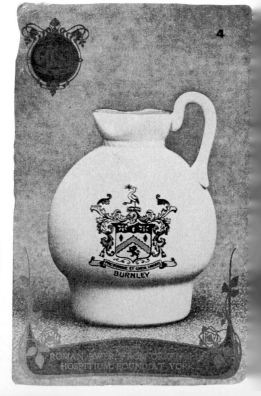

96. Character baby boy doll, 25 in. tall, with bisque head, blue sleeping eyes and composition body. The head is marked K*R Simon and Halbig 116/A. The doll wears its original Norfolk jacket in blue linen embroidered in herringbone stitch. *Courtesy of Christie's South Kensington.*

97. Talking doll, Bébé Jumeau Phonographique, 26 in. tall, with bisque head, fixed eyes and composition body, which contains a Lioret phonograph movement, with celluloid cylinder. This plays 'Petite mère, écoute ma chanson' and other cylinders were available. The very rare phonograph was first made in 1900 and the doll dates from shortly after this. It has its original clothes and box with instructions. *Courtesy of Christie's South Kensington.*

98. Teddy bear, about 1912
19 in. tall, of fawn fur fabri
with beige felt paws an
movable head and legs. Th
fabric of the muzzle is clippe
to simulate the natural sho
hair and the nose embroidere
in black. The bear unlace
down the front to contai
a tin hot water bottle. Thoug
agreeably warm, he was to
big to be cuddled co
veniently and consequentl
the fur is hardly worn. *In t*
collection of Miss Alison Kell

99. Wild West models by William Britain. An illustration from t
firm's catalogue of about 1910. Best known for their toy soldier
this firm also made vivid miniatures of footballers, scouts, etc. Thi
at five shillings, was a comparatively expensive set. *Courtesy of Mes*
Britains Ltd.

fans. These had an elegance seldom seen in the long trailing single plumes and sprays of the 1920s.

A collector's byway is the Edwardian novelty fan that tried to be useful with much the effect one might expect of such butterfly creatures. A few continued the traditional notion of a mirror or spyglass in guard or rivet. But more ambitious notions of around 1900 were found in Walter Thornhill's patent dressing case fans. According to Mrs de Vere Green the idea may have come from Dame Madge Kendal. Swivelling covers concealed hollows in the black, wooden, battoir-shaped guards to contain such items as mirror, glove hook, comb, scissors, hairpins, needle and thread. A tiny vinaigrette or silver powder box and puff might fit one widened guard shoulder and the tassel bob was a thimble case. This firm covered a wide range of crafts in silversmithing and cutlery to fit out their dressing cases and fans and supply 'latest novelties for wedding presents'.

Most Edwardians resorted instead to handbags. These might be of the usual purse style in leather or of a dress-matching fabric in a drawstring 'Dorothy'. Gold and silver chain bags were popular but silver quickly stained white gloves if not frequently washed with ammonia. The chatelaine that had carried a collection of tiny necessities for so many centuries was nearly (though not quite) forgotten while the name lingered on into the new century in the chatelaine bag, a pouched bag in silk or velvet closed at the top with an ornate metal clasp. Attached was a sturdy chain topped by a matching hook for fixing it to the belt. Apprehensive travellers might wear leather versions inside their cloaks or wraps.

Another popular silver detail at the waist was a hook for hanging a pencil case. The firm of S. Mordan and Company, manufacturing silversmiths of City Road, London E.C., has left its name on many minor Edwardian collectables such as smelling bottles and match boxes, and they made their own embossing presses for shaping their products. But their ever-pointed pencil was their particular pride: their telegraphic address was merely 'Pencils'.

Perfume was so important to Edwardians that delicately scented fans, appropriately flower-painted, were only to be expected of the renowned Rimmel perfumiers of Regent Street and other London addresses. This followed the centuries-old tradition of gracing gifts with fragrance, although surely most recipients would have their own preferred perfumes ready bottled and to hand for all occasions. One of the chatelaine's last duties was to provide easy access to both reassuring sweetness and pungent smelling salts.

Here, too, the Edwardians continued Victorian notions with

innumerable small bottles impossible to date unless by silver hallmarks on their heavily embossed covers. Some were in costly jewelled gold or silver, cold smooth jade or smoky rock crystal. But far more were in glass, some in willow pattern china, to continue the story of 'handkerchief scents' carried in handbag, muff or glove, along with toilet waters on the dressing table and scented smelling salts to hand for all emergencies. Design ranged from inch-high hearts and egg shapes for hanging on chatelaine or sautoir to massive silver and cut glass toilet flasks locked in the openwork frame known as a tantalus.

After more than a century of flattened pear shapes the hand bottles were most frequently shaped like a fob watch or an inverted pear tapering to a point at the bottom. More imaginative designs included bird and bird's-head outlines, some in cased glass. Many other glass bottles were deeply cut to insulate them a little from heat that would evaporate the precious contents. Others were harnessed in embossed silver, mostly in all-over scrolling patterns.

The double-ended union bottle was an enduring favourite. A substantial tube, sometimes as much as 7 inches long and 6 ounces in weight, was formed by fusing two bottles base to base. One half would be filled with a flowery handkerchief scent, the other with smelling salts based on invigorating, but quickly dissipated ammonia and made fragrant with attars of lavender, bergamot, rosemary and cloves. Many of these, too, were of thick, deeply cut glass, some richly coloured, or of glass-lined silver or nickel alloy; others of flower-painted china.

The lids at the ends might be press embossed but the essential was that they should be distinctly different. Usually one was hinged to spring open at a touch on a small stud: this was for the smelling salts. Inside the lid was a glass-covered disc controlled by a hidden spring so that when closed the small vessel was entirely sealed from spilling the crystal salts. At the other end a screw cap covered a glass stopper —occasionally a cork—securing the handkerchief scent.

A delightful find is a union bottle that is hinged in the middle where the two bottles meet, offering a tiny cache, for a locket photograph perhaps. Some of these, too, were by the prolific S. Mordan and Company. Other makers whose names may be found include Maw, Son and Thompson (S. Maw and Son by 1911) and the Regent Street silversmith-jewellers Howell and James, whose interest covered clocks, lace, silks, and the period's ubiquitous dressing cases.

Another collectable item carried by the well-to-do Edwardian resulted from the extraordinary little ritual known as leaving cards. This continued far into the 1920s—and what perils of ill manners passed with its abandonment. As 'Au Fait' in one of my etiquette books points out 'it is idle to expect to find anyone at home during the calling hours [mid-afternoon, although known as morning calls] but calls are made nevertheless and cards are left'. Indeed this was the intention, a first tentative approach towards friendship that could be welcomed or rebuffed without loss of dignity by the following move in the delicate game—always assuming that the servant at the door kept a faithful record and the cards were preserved on their status-symbol hall-trays.

By definition a lady could not be rude unintentionally but woe betide the inept who broke the implicit rules. It was all too easy to become confused even though her own cards were always larger than her husband's. The tentative words *To enquire* added to a card served as a delicate forerunner of today's cheerful get-well greetings.

By Edwardian days the engraved cards had long lost their early gloss and flourished lettering but they still required elegant cases. Here was something that the Victorians and Edwardians did to perfection in a dozen different materials, such as most popular tortoiseshell and parquet patterns in mother-of-pearl (which could be personally inscribed, but at twice the cost of silver engraving). Edwardian hall-marks on silver cases sometimes indicate a continuation of the Victorian's slim shape, about four inches tall by three inches wide. Typically this has a deep cover opening on a tiny three-lug hinge on one edge when a spring stud is pressed on the other, these edges being less than half an inch wide.

The vulnerable hinge and fastening persisted throughout my period, and some early cigarette cases continued its inbuilt weakness. Ornament included all-over flower patterns, figure scenes, views and many Japanese themes. Often plain surfaces were covered with finger-pleasing, geometrical patterns of lines known as engine turning to avoid the shame of showing finger marks. But that narrow hinge was so weak that sensible Edwardians usually preferred the wallet style with the hinge all down one side, like a book.

Inevitably this offered opportunities for 'improvements'. Some cases fan open to reveal a dozen little blue silk compartments. Others are found fitted with memo tablet and propelling pencil or extra pockets for postage stamps or a perpetual calendar. Many of these are of Russian leather, crocodile, lizard, morocco, either stiff or limp, their precious metal restricted to 9 carat gold or silver corners, suitably rounded to cause and suffer minimal wear in handbag or pocket instead of being carried in impeccably gloved fingers.

Edwardian silver and leather cigar and cigarette cases tended to be equally sensible, often curved to lessen pocket bulge, the silver ribbed or engine turned. But for the minority seeking elegance a spectacular example was offered by the Fabergé establishment in white, green and red golds ribbed and fluted to perfection. In some cases the patterned metal was entirely covered in translucent enamel—yellow over gold perhaps or lilac over silver—with an immaculate hinge and a tiny thumbpiece gem. Fabergé gold marked 56 equals our 14 carat; silver marked 88 or 84 is a little below sterling quality. H. C. Bainbridge, Fabergé's admiring biographer, remembered great royal patronage of the Dover Street showrooms, even one late afternoon when Queen Alexandra 'brought with her the King and Queen of Norway, the King of Greece, the King of Denmark . . . "May we open the drawers?" the Queen asked'. Mid-Edwardians still bought match-and-tinder boxes, but the tinder rope, or the hole for it, and the extra compartment for matches put many a Fabergé case out of fashion once petrol lighters came in during the war.

Edward VII added to his collection of cigar lighters with a Fabergé hippopotamus in nephrite. But everyday smokers made do with attractive little vesta boxes. Vestas were safer than earlier matches, phosphorus headed on stems of cotton dipped in paraffin wax. But they would strike on any roughened surface and the cautious smoker carried no more than a few in a tiny gilt-lined metal box, perhaps $1\frac{1}{2}$ by $2\frac{1}{4}$ inches, at once identified today by its serrated strike-panel, usually on the base. Like so many other tiny collectables, from seal to watch-key, it was often looped to swing on the Albert watch chain.

The small size and naive ornament have wide appeal. On silver the hallmarks help the collector to pick out Edwardian work, mainly marked with the Birmingham anchor. Some are inlaid with semi-precious stones such as souvenirs patterned with Scotch pebbles or with shamrocks of Connemara marble. Others are in fancy shapes from violin to brandy flask, from enamelled old boot to man-in-the-moon. Frequently these are in electroplate or base-metals; others are in ivory or glass. But here is an almost limitless subject that can be extended to table boxes and lidless match holders such as the china figure fairings with matches at their backs. All were only slowly ousted by the case that enclosed wooden safety matches in their own maker's box. The case had a cutaway side to expose the strip of special material required for striking. Several Edwardian firms made safety matches but even the familiar Bryant and May still made a range of earlier favourites, including vestas. Glass match-strikers were among the 'penny goods' advertised by Joseph Kidd of Manchester in 1905.

Even vesta boxes incorporated some strange, multi-purpose notions such as might be expected of a generation that could pair a pencil with a champagne swizzle stick. A vesta box might carry a knife and pencil, or sovereigns, or serve as a whistle. Many, such as the popular champagne bottle shape in nickel, ivory or horn, included a cigar cutter. Such cutters were often of silver, the basic design suggesting a pocket knife—some 'improved' designs were tubular—with a cup-shaped recess at one end for notching the cigar. Here again was an Edwardian watch-chain detail especially dear at a time when even a cufflink might be shaped as a cigar complete with enamelled band and ash tip, linked by chain to an enamelled vesta.

For Edwardian women, softly nestling chiffon and curling plumes only gradually yielded to practical dictates. Feather boas uncurled into bedraggled misery in the rain, but what we remember is not the wide-spreading, long-stemmed umbrella but the period's dignified sunshades. Rheumatic illness in 1867 left Queen Alexandra with a slight limp. Heartened by royal example every sufferer in the country could lean on an elegant walking stick or equally convenient sunshade, some 36 to 40 inches long. Collectors approve of all today, not only for the careful finish given to the working parts but for their delightful handles.

Here again Carl Fabergé set a splendidly extravagant example with knobs of surface-patterned gold under clear enamel, twinkling with rose diamonds, or nephrite carved in rococo scrolls and set with glowing garnets. He, too, enjoyed the period's special fondness for

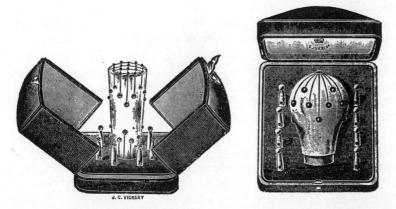

J. C. VICKERY

'Sunshade and entoutcas *handles' shown in 'cases complete with gilt tips for mounting'*
—these being in rock crystal studded with rubies, priced six guineas and four guineas.
From The Connoisseur, *December 1907.*

[91]

crutch heads carved as reptiles with flashing diamond or ruby eyes. Every Edwardian nursery, surely, must have been visited on occasion by a long necked, drake-head sunshade, and there were realistic fruit shapes too. This was an endearing period trait found on ladies' and children's sunshades and umbrellas in silver, ebony, greenhorn and partridge cane. But in more formal shapes of ball, crutch and hook these handles range through gold and silver, rock crystal and ivory, porcelain, mother-of-pearl, amber, tortoiseshell, pigskin and rhinoceros horn. A cased set consisted of a handle and eight matching spoke tips.

The gentleman sported a malacca cane for daytime calls (etiquette demanding that he take it, with hat and gloves, into the drawing room, to indicate his visitor status) and ebony with evening dress. But many other woods were brought in, such as the favourite partridge cane, Brazilian vine, grey crocus wood, pliant lace wood and rugged natural cherry, oak and ash. Cane may be covered throughout with leather; some 'washer sticks' consist of iron cores threading sections of ivory, marbles or other exotics. Henry Howell and Company were important London manufacturers, applying mounts of gold, silver and ivory.

Edwardian bridesmaids frequently carried long, beribboned wands to puzzle us today, but the collector's particular joy, of course, is the ingenious stick concealing a secondary purpose. Swords and daggers are familiar, but what of the pipe, pencil, cigarettes, matchbox, pruning saw, telescope, horse measuring device, even what-the-butler-saw? An electric light might be concealed, or a full-size umbrella. One last delectable reminder of past eccentricities was the Army and Navy Stores' long driving whip with a parasol opening around the stick.

By 1900 umbrella frames such as Fox's Paragon possessed most modern features although as late as 1910 came a Fox patent for a secure arrangement of the rib tips close around the stem. But it is the fabric trimming that makes Edwardian sunshades especially collectable.

The delicacy of the silk and billowing lace prompted charming elaboration of ruched and gathered linings. Ribs and stretchers were thus concealed but even so they might be bound in white lest they showed darkly through a lining of flimsy white. Other parasols were lined in black, but even for mourning the sunshade's black cover and black bow to furnish the bare black handle might be relieved by delicate embroidered detail on insets of translucent silk. Appliquéd braids and perforations produced effective patterns when viewed against a sunny sky. Lace, much of it machine-made, was the ultimate charmer, most often introduced to provide a rich border where the sunshade's main fabric curved inwards between the ribs. Others again had ruchings of semi-transparent chiffon or silk muslin sewn all over the cover and around the edge. No happy spectator at Hurlingham or Henley could wish for more.

10

Embroidery and Lace

EMBROIDERY is such a personal association of art and craft that it could expect a welcome on the Edwardian scene, however mediocre it might have become in mid-Victorian days. In fact it achieved far more. Renewing its age-old magic to transform utility into functional beauty it acquired a place in the thinking and teaching of craftswomen throughout the country that had notable repercussions in the following decades. All this after the Victorians' leisure embroidery had become embroiled in the travesties of Berlin wool work (revived by some Edwardians) and their most exquisite commercial white stitchery was seemingly doomed by machines.

Fascination with Jacobean furnishings around the turn of the century prompted brief vogues for collecting antique embroideries as diverse as pictures, samplers and crewel work hangings. All were worked anew by serious needlewomen and none more eagerly than the crewel stitchery then more pretentiously called art needlework. This suffered the usual disasters of over popularity, with innumerable commercial patterns of sunflowers, briar roses, daffodils and irises, ill-worked on linen and cheaper crash, often in the 'artistic colours' of the faded originals.

By Edwardian days the superb commercial white-on-white costume embroidery known as Ayrshire work was fast losing ground to machine imitations. But for amateur home furnishings the drawn and cut thread work of the Jacobean sampler was widely, although less exquisitely, copied on table runners and chair tidies in somewhat heavy-handed richelieu work. This had cut-away spaces outlined in buttonholing and linked with picot-trimmed bars. Broderie anglaise was even duller, with patterns of stiletto holes, while Rhodes embroidery was flimsier, being pricked with one-eighth-inch hemstitched holes so that it suggested the mottled background of wooden poker work.

The early form of white work known as netting or lacis was recalled in the geometrical patterns darned into squares of plain knotted netting laced to a metal frame. Mrs Isobel Simpson of Edinburgh brought out a book on it in 1909. Edwardians worked it on

Aluminium embroidery on velveteen gown by Fenwick. Lady's Pictorial, *1910.*

machine-woven, shop-prepared net and gave it the grandiose name of guipure d'art. More attractive was the Irish Mountmellick white-on-white, worked on thick, glossy, satin jean. Various thicknesses of white knitting cotton made the most of strongly textured flowers and bramble sprays embroidered in braid, cable, coral, bullion and other bold stitches. But even for this the English fancy-work shop tended to offer weak imitations.

A happier revival was comfortable smocking, albeit for a new middle class indoor setting, while the yet more demanding craft of the quilter survived in several distinctive regional styles.

Ambitious home embroiderers planning portières, screens and the like might apply to the Morris firm, which supplied suitable patterned materials and their own dyed silks to cover them in radiating darned stitches fitting the forms of the richly intertwined leaves and petals. Morris's daughter May was in charge of the firm's needlework department, which also sold magnificent professional embroideries. Morris's own most popular designs for woven tapestry were adapted, such as the *Pomona* and *Flora* figures originally drawn by Burne-Jones and set against more formal verdure backgrounds by the firm's art director J. H. Dearle, 1860–1932.

For many other art-conscious amateur home embroiderers Morris's friend, the silk printer Thomas Wardle, supplied the Leek Embroidery Society (founded by his wife) with tussores and other silks and cottons suitably wood-block printed, together with his own dyed silks for stitching closely over the printed lines. And at the other extreme, needlework magazines, stores such as Whiteleys of Westbourne Grove and innumerable fancy-work shops, following all these trends, offered undemanding transfer patterns and prepared materials, along with immensely popular braids and bugles, beads and jet.

The decorated articles left from this vast amateur endeavour include dress trimmings and accessories, cushions and pin-cushions, lampshades, furniture and bed covers, table runners, tray cloths and cosies, sets of mats for dressing table and wash-stand and every kind of knick-knack from the pocket-shaped hair tidy for hanging by the looking-glass to bead-weighted covers for the bedroom hot water cans.

Much design was banal enough but some caught the flavour of a period not yet embarrassed by make-believe or nursery rhyme. For example, a 'sampler' to celebrate Edward VII's coronation, 23 inches wide by 7 inches deep, was printed with the outlines for five small illustrated panels with motifs from seventeenth-century picture embroideries comparable with their hopefully quaint rhyming captions such as—

> *This is Edwardes*
> *Crowning yeer*
> *See his Crowne*
> *I sew you heer*

This is his Palace
Where he bides
He has many
Moe besides.   and so on.

The design in two sizes printed on linen was made and sold by Miss Strawson of Boston and Woodhall Spa, Lincolnshire, at *Ye Signe of Ye Spindle*. It was so popular that she devised another in the same mood for the coronation of King George V and Queen Mary. This sold for 3s 10d (small size) or 10s 9d with the silks for working it, the designer's father having invented boiling dyes for embroidery silks.

All this, however, is only part of the story. Everywhere more enterprising efforts were beginning to take effect. It says much for their success that leading Edwardian designers accepted commissions from embroiderers—among them Voysey in the airy manner of his wallpapers, Walter Crane, Selwyn Image, M. H. Baillie Scott, Lewis Day, Alexander Fisher.

In 1900 Lewis Day in *Art in Needlework* was still critical of much current embroidery. He saw tent stitch pictorial work as 'even more foolish than a picture in mosaic', and noted that the sweeping lines of chain stitch and far speedier work with the tambour hook were all too easily imitated by the sewing machine. He found a 'stuffy look' about chenille embroidery and referred with distaste to 'flaunting art needle-work' in contrast with 'the delicate work in white on white . . . which makes no loud claim to be art but is content to be beautiful'. The important point was that he saw at that time a readership willing to accept a new, analytical approach to the subject, seeking 'beauty, not novelty'.

Embroidery was thus accepted as an integral part of the movement seeking a finer world through personal, creative craftsmanship, although Walter Crane realized that it was 'a world within a world; a minority producing for a minority'.

It may have been the sheer mediocrity of much art needlework that had prompted the founding of the Royal School of Art Needlework in 1872 where women had to reach a certificated standard of technique to qualify for possible employment.

But by my period the idea had spread country-wide with increasingly skilled amateurs and professionals participating in arts and crafts exhibitions and taking advantage of professional designs, expert tuition and appreciative customers. As yet only a few idealists, such as Day, stressed the need for simple pattern making, created out of an under-standing of materials and stitches. In his needlework book he relied on

[97]

Mary Buckle for the practical work. Other women of this period who encouraged embroiderers to range widely among possible techniques and stitches included the women's magazine editor Flora Klickmann and the fine craftswoman Mrs Archibald Christie.

Some groups, such as the Decorative Needlework Society, under Queen Alexandra's patronage, and the Harris Flax Depot, concentrated on ecclesiastical embroidery. This was entirely in keeping with the period's mood although Day commented that such work might be 'not only the most frigid and rigid in design, but the hardest and most mechanical in execution'. Craft guilds might seek church commissions, such as Bromsgrove, and the Haslemere Peasant Industries. The latter, founded by Godfrey Blount in 1896, supplied church furnishings worked out in appliqué heavily outlined in black like the period's leaded stained glass. In *The Studio*, 1903, Baillie Scott, himself a texture-conscious designer of rich appliqué work, scoffed that these were 'seldom practised by peasants and cannot be strictly described as embroidery'. But Day foresaw a future for appliqué work: 'mere prettiness is beyond its scope; but it lends itself to dignity of design and nobility of treatment. Of course it is not popular.'

Not surprisingly appliqué was particularly important in the movement towards more creative, simple needlework fostered in Glasgow by Jessie R. Newbery, wife of the principal of the School of Art. Mrs Newbery taught needlework and embroidery until 1908 when she was followed by Ann Macbeth, 1875–1948, author of the influential *Educational Needlework*. Here, as in other crafts I have described, the Glasgow C. R. Mackintosh influence was far-reaching. The architect's wife Margaret Macdonald herself designed and worked embroideries associated with his commissions. In Glasgow, embroidery design was as decorative, yet restrained and stylized, as the high-shouldered lettering it frequently included, or the disciplined exaggeration of a Mackintosh chair.

The Studio review of pen drawings, 1900–1, commented that 'women are making a speciality of decoration . . . because decorative penwork is the legitimate descendant of embroidery and the purely feminine arts', and there is perhaps too much of the lettered print about many 'progressive' Edwardian embroideries. It is no surprise to find in Glasgow work an emphasis on black and white, supplemented with pinkish tones and subtle greys, far from the 'greenish blues, the yellows inclining to green or brown' and the 'blacks of a greenish or olive tone' recommended for embroideries by Crane and long pursued by late Victorian aesthetes.

Fig. 89, worked out in linen appliqué and silk embroidery upon

'*Being Took*' *by Edith Farmiloe, illustrator of the period's* Dumpy Books. *The fascination for child drawings among the new school of line artists was praised by Charles Holme, who welcomed the fact that their work could at last be reproduced without the intermediary hand of a wood engraver. Specially drawn for* The Studio, *Winter number 1900–1.*

linen, typically shows the exuberant plant life of *art nouveau* squared up and formalized so that the effect is restrained and two-dimensional. Ann Macbeth, robbed in childhood of normal stereoscopic vision, could design brilliantly rich effects in two-dimensional appliqué, including ecclesiastical work such as a banner of silk and velvet appliqué with silk and cloth of gold for St Bartholomew's Church, Haslemere. Frances Templeton was a notable Glasgow student, and there were others whose designs have been recorded, such as Muriel Boyd. More importantly, many who trained there in turn became teachers, fostering enjoyment of original design and easy stitchery among children far beyond their own generation.

Perhaps the surprise here is that they so easily accepted many of the period's conventions such as the ubiquitous heart shapes and mottoes. A coverlet design by Ann Macbeth shows six lines from Blake's *Auguries of Innocence* 'Joy and woe are woven fine . . . ' using the typical Glasgow high-shouldered lettering and further decorated with six

[99]

formal wild roses and four rows of small hearts. A banal design, perhaps, but complying pleasantly with Mrs Newbery's own most un-Victorian conviction, quoted by Gleeson White: 'I especially aim at beautifully shaped spaces and try to make them as important as the patterns'.

In Birmingham, Mary Newill, 1860–1947, taught embroidery and design through Edwardian days and contributed to the Bromsgrove Guild. A coverlet designed and made in 1908 shows a formalized pattern illustrating lines from Wordsworth beginning 'The rainbow comes and goes' lettered around its edge.

In Edinburgh, a brilliant embroiderer in the period's arts and crafts mood was Dublin-trained Phoebe Traquair, 1852–1936, wife of the keeper of Edinburgh's Science and Art Museum. In *Historical Needlework* Margaret Swain takes up again the fascinating story of white embroidery in Scotland told in *The Flowerers*, and observes that 'perhaps the most outstanding needlewoman of recent times was Lady Evelyn Stuart Murray, 1863–1940'. Her 'undoubted masterpiece' was a panel worked in about 1912 in fine white cotton upon cambric displaying the Royal Arms within a richly scrolling border decorated with roses, thistles and shamrock flanking the Prince of Wales's feathers and motto. Here, as in the finest Ayrshire work, the embroiderer included exquisite pulled fabric fillings, the cambric gathered by the stitching into a range of tiny openwork patterns suggesting needlepoint lace. Other remembered needlewomen include Christine Angus, wife of the artist Sickert, and Emile Lessore's grand-daughter Elaine.

The improvement in embroidery techniques was only part of the purpose behind the Royal School and many other needlework societies. The Embroiderers' Guild founded in 1906 emphasized at the time that its aim was instruction and advice for the highly skilled, but more typical were the many guilds and associations whose annual bazaars were recorded each December in the press. Here the aim was largely to find work for needy gentlewomen. Barbara Morris in her book *Victorian Embroidery* includes a list of those at work near the end of her period.

Throughout Edwardian days the Working Ladies Guild, for example, remained important, patronized by royalty and selling embroideries along with so-called marquetery staining, gesso and pewter work. The Home Arts and Industries Association brought together saleable items from many regions. In 1913, for example, they could still offer knitting from Curraghmore and the Orkneys and Shetlands, lace from North Buckinghamshire, Honiton and Norfolk and gold and silver lace from Berkshire, silk embroideries and drawn thread work on linen from the Countess of Bessborough's Garryhill peasant industry, spun silks from Annie Garnett's Windermere spinnery, elaborate, woven silks and woollens from the London School of Weaving, tweeds and homespuns from Stonehenge. All this as well as pottery, leather, wood veneers, metalwork, enamels, artificial flowers, dressed dolls and rugs.

It was noted in *The Queen* that the Essex and North Riding groups had 'lately been affiliated to the older society, the work of which seems now to extend into almost every part of the United Kingdom'. This included Scotland, with such groups as the Wemyss Castle School, and the Donegal Industrial Fund with its renowned Kells embroidery.

Some of these groups were immensely important in reviving really skilled craftwork such as drawn thread work designed by a Mrs Pepper for the Langdale branch. The Berkshire work mentioned above came from embroiderers of Kingston-Bagpuize taught by Mrs Lessing. Fisherton-de-la-Mere in Wiltshire gave its name to another successful 'industry' established there in 1902 by an embroidery teacher Mrs Arthur Newall, largely dependent on traditional Italian counted-thread patterns. The Hertford School of Embroidery was yet another group, covering embroideries as diverse as vellum bookcovers and handker- chief monograms.

Just how wretched the pay might be for the hard-pressed Edwardian needlewoman may be realized from prices quoted in *The Queen* in 1911 for plain sewing by the Church Army needlework department: for the period's voluminous night gowns, 2s, chemises, knickers, bodices, 1s, white petticoats, 1s 6d, and 'flannelette underclothing is cheaper'. Yet the *Girl's Own Annual* in 1913 noted that many fashionable women owned eight to twelve hats at £5 to £10 each and some would run through twice that outlay in a season. While dress remained *the* status symbol, overdressing was inevitable, as were also the poorer girl's imitations, often shabby before the payments-by-instalments were complete. (Even the wealthy lady's pathetic osprey plumes were imitated, in grass and horsehair, until a new awareness of cruelty came into the story.)

In the *Daily News* Sweated Trades Exhibition, 1906, nineteen out of the thirty-two trades shown were concerned with costume, and nearly all might so well have been delightful tasks if conditions had been better—beadwork, military embroidery, shawl fringing, umbrella covering, artificial flower-making and the like. Yet even the poorly paid sewing woman might be remembered as a 'rosy cheeked tubby little woman who was full of fun and told the most entrancing stories' while paying her annual spring visit of a month or more to work through a household's year-long accumulation of sewing jobs. That expert on costume and needlework Mrs Mary Ireland remembers such visits to her childhood home for all that they taught her. (And remembers too the hurried costume changes that followed Victoria's death. Her mother wore nothing but black for almost six months while she as a nine year old was let off with half-mourning violet outfit.) Her costume for village lessons until old enough for boarding school included a cloth dress with a fine crochet collar and a pinafore of Chinese or Japanese silk befrilled at neck, hem and armholes with yards of valenciennes lace.

This was a remarkable period for exquisite frillies including fantastic blouses and embroidered, beribboned lingerie, in contrast to the cloth coats and dresses loaded with heavy buttons and coiling braid. The blouse especially was magnificent, with a high boned collar and delicate trimmings all down a front that was pouched over the shirt waist band. Alison Adburgham in *Shops and Shopping* notes that Bond Street's White House in 1906 offered a laundry service. This in a London where in 1913 someone calculated that upwards of 150 tons of soot was produced daily 'and hangs over us in smoke—55,000 tons a year'.

Trimmings included glass beads, often dyed to match their setting or jewel brilliant in enamel colours, and all manner of ruffles, tucks, pleats and insertions of machine-made lace. So-called chemical lace with its somewhat solid, lumpy, 'seventeenth-century Venetian point' style particularly suited the early Edwardian mood. This was made by embroidery machine on a ground of a different fibre that could be dissolved away.

Breaking away from the early Edwardian's gentle colours, the later years' bizarre styles introduced heavy embroidery 'replete with Eastern reminiscences' and 'in kaleidoscopic colours of barbaric splendour' to quote comments from as early as 1907. Some of the ubiquitous beadwork was applied even to delicate voiles. In 1911 *The Queen* noted 'the determined suppression of embroidery, especially bead broderie' and the none-too-happy substitution of dyed lace, but the embroidery vogue continued.

Susan, Lady Tweedsmuir, in *The Edwardian Lady* recollected how Edwardians 'tried to revive old and faded dresses with bits of lace, chiffon, tulle, which in fact did not succeed in doing anything except give the dress in question a slightly messy and muddled appearance . . . We must have bought literally miles of the kind of bead trimmings called passementerie with which to renovate ageing dresses.'

To judge by women's magazines, however, one would think that the Edwardians' main preoccupation was with crochet (and tatting for the shortsighted). Crochet was so popular in the craft schools in Ireland, where there was no long tradition of lace making, that in Paris it became known as Irish point. Edwardians also favoured other Irish lace substitutes, such as the somewhat frail Carrickmacross appliqué, widely taught in the work schools. This used intricate patterns embroidered on muslin or cambric, cut out and stitched on machine-made net. An obvious alternative also found at this time was speedy embroidery either chain-stitched on the net with a tambour hook or needle-run in darning stitches. Both might figure in 'Limerick lace'.

Some of this needle-run work was called lace, too, on the Isle of Wight and indeed, apart from obvious Irish motifs, the Irish is indistinguishable from similar English work. 'Tape lace' was yet another popular imitation, with needle-worked fillings to link patterns shaped in machine-made braid.

None of these really disguised the fact that the netted mesh lay under the decorative motifs rather than being built around them as in real lace. Carrickmacross guipure, with no net ground to support the embroidered cambric motifs, was flimsier still and soon frayed with the pull of the linking needlepoint bars.

The tambour work referred to above deserves more than passing notice as the Edwardians' love of transparent fabrics prompted its re-emergence for speedy and effective decoration. It was created by hand with a short steel hook, not too sharp, screwed into an ivory or bone handle often containing a tube for needles. This worked patterns in a running chain stitch on machine-made net or other thin fabric stretched on a circular 'tambour frame'. Even large items were quickly decorated, such as shawls, court trains and bridal veils. During my period it was included among the country craftwork widely displayed by Liberty's, being supplied by the Essex Tambour Lace Industry of Coggeshall, then the only source. By unconfirmed tradition Coggeshall white work can be recognized by the bold patterns composed of closely covered round dots.

Highly esteemed lace was made in Ireland during my period but on a small scale. Fine needlepoint from the north was included in Queen Alexandra's coronation robe as a tucker veiled with gold lace. This was Innismacsaint lace, based on Venetian rose point, a venture started in the 1860s when crochet was out of favour, and the style was copied in Co. Waterford. For a time Youghal had its Co-operative Lace Society and some bobbin lace was made at the Presentation Convent, but even here Mrs Head observed in *The Lace and Embroidery Collector*, 1922, the craft had largely given way to crochet. All sold well to the Edwardians, the long tradition of pitifully low rates of piecework pay often giving them the edge over Continental laces.

Mrs Gaskell's wedding gown, going-away costume and bridesmaids' dress. From The Queen, *8 February 1902.*

Even the English lace maker, under philanthropic supervision, derived some benefit when the general upsurge in creative handwork coincided with the Edwardians' unprecedented love of lace, ranging from heavy tape laces for dresses to the most ethereal for blouse and hat trimming. Honiton appliqué and guipure had their ups and downs. At the beginning of my period a Honiton appliqué shawl might cost £14 and 16-inch deep flouncing was nearly £3 a yard. A Taunton Honiton lace class was started in 1902.

Patricia Wardle in *Victorian Lace* refers to A. Penderel Moody's description in 1907 of local Honiton lace agencies where commissions were placed with the cottagers at so much a motif, haphazardly put together to make up the required price. But Mrs Head noted better designs for the flower motifs, made in finer stitching, less slackly worked although the thread and hence the texture might still be poor. In 1922 she reported that 'some nice lace had been produced of late years' and this was confirmed in *The Queen*, 1913, with praise for Miss Lancaster Lucas's lace industry at Shaldon. At Beer and Seaton, too, Honiton's many filling stitches were revived and its varied grounds of bars and bobbin-made net.

By then the Midlands Lace Association was employing several hundred workers and in North Buckinghamshire Miss Kewley supervised the making of fans, scarves and handkerchiefs. On a small scale Maltese lace was made in this region, Mrs Head contrasting the characteristic ovals in Maltese work with the English ovals, square ended and seldom arranged as a Maltese cross.

Some of the most interesting English Edwardian lace was made by the Diss Lace Association, Norfolk, where the craft was introduced about 1902, employing some 50 workers by 1912. Here for very many years the indefatigable organizer and teacher was Miss Alice Savory. The Honiton styles were followed, the widely varied hand-made net and bar backgrounds contributing to the richness of the patterns. In 1913 the group could boast that they (and not Honiton) had been chosen to send a teacher to launch the industry in North Devon.

---===✦ 11 ✦===---

Paper and Print

by *Alison Kelly*

THIS chapter, concerned with printing and paper, ranges from the most trivial ephemera to serious artistic achievements. As it is often the unconsidered trifles which best characterize the age, we will begin with the trivia.

Cigarette cards began as small bits of cardboard to stiffen the paper covers of cigarette packets, and by the 1880s were decorated with lithographed pictures. By Edwardian times manufacturers were including sets of *Country Seats* (1906), *British Costume* (1904), *Kings and Queens* (1902 and 1911), aspects of the *South African War*, *Nelson* (1905) and so on. Normally there were fifty cards in a set, but the longest running series (1894–1906) was of *Actresses and Beauties*, and contained 4,000 cards. These were photographs, not the usual lithographs; other unusual media were satin, for a set of *Moths and Butterflies*, and silk for a set of *Flowers*.

A larger item of decorative printing was the postcard; a cheap postal rate for cards and a relaxation in the regulations which had previously limited them to 3½ inches were the two factors which came together to produce the postcard mania of the Edwardian period. Even so, until 1903 the sender was faced with two inconvenient alternatives; one side was reserved for the address, so that the other side had to have either a small vignette which left space for a note to be written round its edges, or a large picture with no room for a message; it was the French who first thought of putting both message and address on the same side of the card.

Raphael Tuck was among the first to establish a large business in cards, their Oilette series, with a finish suggesting oil paints, being especially popular. Other large firms were Valentine of Dundee and Wrench, who photographed art collections; but there were very many small producers of postcards, since every town had its jobbing printer producing cards of local beauty spots.

It soon became the fashion to make up albums of cards and, to satisfy collectors, cards were often issued in sets, usually with six in a set. The variety was enormous, and in 1905 there was even an *Illustrated Daily Postcard*, with a heading in Gothic type like a newspaper, and an item of news. Current events were illustrated—a plane crash, the Sydney Street Siege—and patriotic cards came in with the 1914 War. Comic cards abounded, with the eternal subjects of henpecked husbands and mothers-in-law. Louis Wain, in about 1905, produced the first of his comedy cats, a subject which occupied him so exclusively that in later life he went mad and retired to a cat-phantasmagoria. Another one-subject artist was Charles Dana Gibson, whose Gibson girl, in S-bend poses which now seem to defy anatomy, represented the ideal of Edwardian charm. His first designs date from 1903.

Apart from lithography and photography, experiments were made in other media. Stevens of Coventry made woven silk Stevengraph 'cards'. Satin, tinsel and sequins were stuck on cards, and Spanish beauties were shown in embroidered gauze shawls. Feathers and paper lace could be added, particularly for valentine postcards, which were now more popular than the older valentine discreetly enclosed in an envelope. Trick cards abounded, with hidden transparencies, sections which revolved, and messages which could be washed off, leaving another below.

The postcard, though it reflected most aspects of Edwardian life, gives us very little idea of the art influences of the time. Alphonse Mucha designed some cards about 1901, but otherwise *art nouveau* does not seem much reflected in postcards, and the arts and crafts movement does not seem to have produced the number of woodcuts, etchings and other hand-printed cards which might have been expected. For this aspect of the Edwardian world we have to turn to the poster, the art magazine and the private press book.

It was in the Edwardian decade that the *Connoisseur* (1901), for the study of paintings, furniture and *objets d'art*, and the *Burlington Magazine* (1903), which concentrated on art historical research, joined the *Studio* (in its early days a very *avant garde* publication, much influenced by *art nouveau*) which was founded in 1894. All three flourish today, but three, typical of their period, foundered after short runs. *The Page*, edited by Edward Gordon Craig and mainly including his own work, with some Beerbohm and Rothenstein drawings, ran from 1898 to 1901. *The Acorn*, reflecting arts and crafts trends, ran from 1905 to 1906, and *Rhythm*, edited by Middleton Murry and his wife Katherine Mansfield, on art and literature, came out between 1911 and 1913.

Victorian posters had been uninspiring, being either masses of ill-designed lettering or reproductions of Academy-type paintings. The Beggarstaff Brothers (actually William Nicholson and his brother-in-law

James Pryde) broke away from these conventions, with experiments in lithography, woodcuts, paper collage and other media to produce bold, contrasting patterns. Their sense of humour was delightful, and comedy can also be seen in the posters of the cartoonist Phil May, whose quick, expressive line shows us girls of bedraggled vivacity advertising drinks that they have clearly enjoyed too often. Walter Crane was also an illustrator, much influenced by *art nouveau*; the sinuous, elongated shapes of this style appear in his book illustrations and on a larger scale in his posters.

Crane was more at home on a smaller scale, however, whereas poster size came more naturally to the etcher Frank Brangwyn. This artist, when not painting huge murals, produced some of the largest etchings ever made. Not particularly influenced by any of the art styles of his time, his great rugged compositions have a drama of their own which could be adapted for posters, particularly striking examples being for First World War charities. Those commissioning his etchings as posters showed that unconventional techniques were becoming acceptable, in place of traditional realism.

New ideas were also appearing in typography, as well as in pictorial design, and not before they were needed. As part of the long divorce of art from crafts, Victorians had been insensitive to lettering. William Morris, however, with his fascinated interest in crafts of all kinds, had begun to design and print books in the 1890s, during the last few years of his life, and his Kelmscott editions greatly influenced typographical designers at the beginning of the new century. Gradually artists in various allied media began to consider the forms of letters and their composition on the page, and a whole group of presses were founded to produce books as works of art.

These, like Morris's, were private presses, since it was accepted that such enterprises could not be commercial successes. The texts were usually poetry and often obscure, and were in Latin and Italian as well as English. The editions were often minute; the Essex House Press *Courtier* by Castiglione is in an edition of only 200 copies, and some had as few as fifty. Attempts at producing a consciously beautiful book sometimes resulted in a work which was easier to look at than to read; Morris had been influenced by early 'black-letter' printing, and liked decorated borders and foliated capitals on a dense-looking page, with little spacing between words and lines. All these elements influenced the Edwardian typographers, in some cases too much. The Kelmscott Chaucer is a masterpiece in its own way, but one of it is enough.

The Ashendene Press, first set up in 1895 but continuing into the Edwardian decade, was one of the finest of these private presses.

St John Hornby, its founder, escaped the pervasive Morris influence, basing his type-face on that used by early Italian printers at Subiaco in 1465. Appropriately, Hornby concentrated on Italian and Latin texts, printing Marcus Aurelius and (probably his finest achievement) an edition of Dante. The very large format of this Dante, produced between 1902 and 1905, enhanced the quality of the beautiful Italian type-face. Hornby's books were often enriched with ornaments by the young Eric Gill, Graily Hewitt and Louise Powell, all of them pupils of Edward Johnston, whose classes in lettering at the Central School of Art were probably the most influential this century. Hornby's output was small, but of the highest quality.

The Doves Press began as a book-binding firm in 1894. The art of the book cover was beginning to be as much considered as the letterpress and some fine bindings were produced. In 1900, the Doves Bindery founder, T. J. Cobden Sanderson, set up his press with Emery Walker, who provided the stability of the firm as Cobden Sanderson was an unstable idealist, alternating between euphoria and breakdown. He was passionate about craftsmanship and is said to have originated the phrase 'the art and crafts movement'. The press was emphatically anti-Morris, and the books had no decoration at all, apart from the dignified, calligraphic initial letters by Johnston, which punctuated the Jenson Roman type-face. The Doves Press produced a Bible, some poetry and Goethe's *Sorrows of Werther*, a hero with whom Cobden Sanderson must have felt affinities. In a wilder moment, he threw all the type and punches into the Thames in 1911, an action which finished the press and resulted in a lawsuit with Walker, who still owned part of it.

Charles Ricketts, the decorative artist, had also thrown his fount of type into the Thames in 1903. His books are elaborate, with decorations and borders, of which, like Morris, he was very fond. He had a vivid conception of a book as a unity, with typography, illustration and binding forming a harmonious whole, in 'a conscious aim towards beauty and order'. Perhaps because of this, the effect was rather precious, particularly in his King's Type. He printed much poetry— Browning, Coleridge, Shelley and Shakespeare.

The Eragny Press was founded by Lucien Pissarro and his wife who began by using Ricketts's type, but after 1903 naturally had created their own. They did everything themselves, designing, printing and making the wood blocks for illustrations, and their books have a delightfully homespun coherence. The press was not a commercial success, but they managed to produce editions of Flaubert, Ronsard and Perrault (French authors, as might be expected) and poems by Coleridge and Keats.

C. R. Ashbee, an important figure in the arts and crafts movement, bought two of the Kelmscott presses after Morris's death, thus declaring his allegiance, and set up the Essex House Press, first in east London and later at Chipping Campden. In 1910 he published a book called *The Private Press, a Study in Idealism*, giving details, with illustrations, of all the books he had published up to that date. He printed a number of pamphlets written by himself, some Spenser and Coleridge,

Initial letter from 'The Thirde Book' of the Courtier.

the *Rubaiyat of Omar Khayyam*, the *Courtier* of Count Baldassare Castiglione, and (a surprising choice) *Parentalia*, the book in which Wren's son and namesake describes the life and work of his architect father. Ashbee's personal symbol seems to have been the pink, a flower which appears, suitably or unsuitably, in almost all his books. After 1906, Ashbee handed over production to an Indian, Coomaraswamy, and the books became more and more eastern and esoteric.

So few copies were printed of these private press books that it is easy to miss them unless they are searched for. They are, however, very typical of their period. The seriousness with which these artists tried to recreate the interdependence of design and craftsmanship is wholly admirable, even if the results do not always come up to the aims. At a time when a book was valued only for its text, these private press publishers insisted that the book itself should be worthy of its subject, and a pleasure to look at as well as read. They form a small but important part of the artistic life of their age. Moreover they did influence, indirectly, the production of commercial books. The *Everyman* series, familiar to everyone, would not have had its characteristic title-page if these private presses had not existed; and many other publishers, even if only for business reasons, were persuaded for the first time that the visual aspect of a book was a matter of concern.

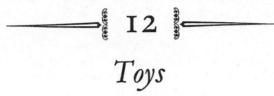

Toys

by *Alison Kelly*

THE late Victorian age changed slowly into the world of the Edwardians and the toy world followed suit. There was no abrupt difference
between the contents of the Victorian and Edwardian nursery cupboard;
clockwork toys, dolls, doll's houses and furniture, soldiers, Noah's
arks all developed slowly, and were alike before and after 1900. The
more dramatic change was in soft toys, and it will be to these that we
shall return in a moment, after considering the more traditional
playthings.

Dolls, over the centuries, have been the special toy of little girls, and
the Edwardian doll, being more robust than the delicate, waxen-faced,
Victorian beauty, could be played with more satisfactorily. By the end
of the nineteenth century, the heads of the better dolls were made of
bisque (biscuit porcelain) which could be tinted with ceramic colours
to give a permanent naturalistic complexion. The pink-and-white
colouring of many Edwardian dolls is hardly impaired after seventy
years.

These heads were made with eye sockets for glass eyes, and the more
expensive dolls had 'sleeping' eyes fringed with a luxuriance of eyelashes hardly matched until the invention of the stick-on eyelashes of the
1960s. Bodies for the larger dolls were often of papier-mâché, a strong
amalgam of shredded paper and glue, painted with pink enamel. Legs
and arms which moved only at shoulder and hip joints could also be
of papier-mâché, but where extra movement was required at wrist,
elbow or knee, the limbs had to be carved from wood, with ball and
socket joints. Walking dolls had been manufactured from Victorian
times, and still were after 1900, though never really satisfactorily, and
dolls had been able to say a metallic 'Ma-Ma' for generations; but it
was the invention of the gramophone which allowed the genuinely
talking doll to be made. From 1900, there was a phonograph small
enough to be placed in the doll's stomach, so that she could sing
several little songs.

Though the most elegant dolls had come from France during the nineteenth century, and the Jumeau firm was still world-famous, the Edwardian doll trade was dominated by Germany. Simon and Halbig was one of the most important firms, not only producing complete dolls but also supplying heads for others. It was the practice to use back-stamps on the heads, and SH for Simon Halbig, for instance, can be found combined with KR for Kammer and Reinhardt, or with Jutta, the brand-name of the firm of Drossel. The apparently French name of Armand Marseille was in fact that of a German firm at Koppelsdorf.

The faces reflected fashionable taste; cheeks were plump, mouths small and eyes enormous. The expression, it must be said, was generally vacuous. Kammer and Reinhardt did on one occasion turn towards realism, producing a baby doll with a skinny little face puckered up as if it would cry at any moment, and said to have been modelled from the sculptor's own six-weeks-old baby, but most baby dolls were placid, those from Armand Marseille being particularly engaging.

Though many Victorian dolls were modelled and dressed as adults, the more typical Edwardian doll seems to have been modelled to represent a child of seven or eight, in the same costume as its owner. She often wore a pinafore of white cotton trimmed with broderie anglaise, with drawers and petticoat to match, and so her doll had the same. These can easily be washed, and whereas a doll dressed in silk or velvet now looks faded and sad, one wearing a newly-laundered pinafore, her face sponged and her hair combed, can look almost as fresh as she did when new.

A quite different type of bisque doll was the Kewpie, invented in 1909 by an American illustrator, Rose O'Neill. The name is a coy variant on *cupid*, and she drew these little putti in all sorts of attitudes in a children's strip cartoon. This was so popular that she modelled a prototype and had copies made in J. D. Kestner's German factory. The Kewpie has a large head, bald except for an upstanding quiff of hair, a round tummy and a saccharine expression which its designer no doubt called cute.

Such dolls were too big to live in doll's houses, and there was a small breed of doll, usually all china, or with a china head and stuffed body, made to inhabit them. The doll's house, copying the latest architectural fashions, and typically, at this date, of bright red brick with gables and white paintwork, afforded endless opportunities for the devoted present-giver, since every kind of household equipment —furniture, china, silver, batterie-de-cuisine—could be bought in miniature. Even food could be provided to equip the kitchen and dining-room, and Edwardian children read of the disappointment of

Beatrix Potter's *Two Bad Mice*, who took up residence in a doll's house, and sadly discovered that the succulent hams, puddings and vegetables they had come to eat were nothing but plaster, cleverly painted. Methods of making these miniatures changed little from Victorian times until the age of plastics, so that dating is best done by comparing them with the furniture and equipment shown in Edwardian photographs.

Dolls and their houses had been playthings for generations, but three toys in particular characterized the Edwardian nursery, the teddy-bear, the golliwog and the Dutch, or wooden, doll. Of these, the Dutch doll was a mere revival; Queen Victoria had had a whole family of little carved wooden dolls of minimal realism, with bullet heads and shiny painted hair. Their renewed popularity came from a series of children's books by Florence Upton about the adventures of two Dutch dolls and a golliwogg (her spelling). The latter toy reflects the curious taste of the time which produced the Chocolate-Coloured Coon and the Nigger Minstrels of the seaside concert party. The toy, like the blacked-up singers, was a great success; and Debussy, in *Jeux d'Enfants*, wrote him the charming, syncopated *Golliwog's Cake Walk* which has retained its popularity ever since. The golliwog was a soft toy, made of material and stuffed with rags or sawdust. He had a black face on which his features were embroidered, and hair made of loops of wool. He wore a neat Eton collar and bow tie, and a gaily coloured coat and trousers, following the illustrations in the books.

The fashion for golliwogs has waned in a more ethnically conscious age, but the teddy-bear is still as much a part of the nursery as he was in the 1900s. He owes his name to President Theodore (Teddy) Roosevelt, who was once said to have refrained from shooting a bear-cub because it was on the other side of a State-line. The incident prompted a cartoon, in 1903, called *Teddy's bear*. An enterprising toymaker called Michtom made a stuffed bear-cub and asked permission from the President to call it Teddy's bear. The apostrophe was soon dropped, but the teddy-bear has been with us ever since; it filled the need for an endearing soft toy to take to bed, a rôle inadequately filled by the doll with its cold limbs and hard china face. Good fur-cloths were available, and seductive bears were made from the first. The principal features, movable head, arms and legs, were as now, though early bears were sometimes more detailed. The muzzle was usually more projecting and bear-like in the earlier models, with the fur-fabric clipped to represent the natural short hair. Small bits of suède-finished wool were sewn on to represent the pads on the bear's paws, and sometimes the claws were indicated by lines of stitching. Most

Edwardian bears are now in poor condition, having been embraced almost to extinction.

While Michtom claimed credit for inventing the *teddy*-bear, German toy-historians claim that jointed toy animals, including bears, had already been made by Margarete Steiff. She was an invalid who first made stuffed toys to amuse small friends, and was so successful at it that by 1900 she had established her own exporting business. Her trademark was *Knopf im Ohr*, a button in the ear, and all her toys originally had this detail. She reacted against the insipid prettiness of the bisque-headed dolls, and another German designer, Käthe Kruse, also introduced naturalism, designing stuffed dolls in washable materials. Though she embarked on large-scale production, she prided herself on slight variations between one doll and another, due to the amount of hand work in them. Like Margarete Steiff, she chose an odd place to put her trademark, the inside of the left foot.

So far, most of the toys described have been for little girls. For little boys, who all wanted to be engine drivers, the preferred toy was the train. Clockwork toy trains, to wind up, had first been made in the United States as early as 1856, but the real trains of the day were mostly powered by steam, and it was a model steam train which the small boy coveted. In the 1890s, toy train manufacture was centred in Nuremberg, and the trains copied were those running on European railways, but at the Paris exhibition of 1900 Bassett Lowke met Stefan Bing of Nuremberg, and got him to make models of trains on British lines. The Black Prince engine appeared in 1901, Midland Railway models in 1902, and South Western models in 1903. All were an enormous success, the technical problems of model-scale steam engines being solved by Bassett Lowke's engineer friend Smithies.

Electricity was in use for some railways by the end of the nineteenth century, and of course model trains followed suit. First made in the U.S.A. in 1897, they were in Europe the next year. A Frenchman, Georges Carette, in Nuremberg, made all three types, clockwork, steam and electric, and his models are said to have been the most accurate of all; Bassett Lowke, however, had the cream of the British trade, though the average child had to be content with the cheap, lithographed tinplate, clockwork train from Nuremberg. The admirable Hornby train, solid and very well modelled, did not make its appearance until 1915, at a time when German models were unobtainable. Hornby had, however, produced the ingenious Meccano, with which the Edwardian child could make his own versions of the great engineering achievements of the day, as early as 1901. It is interesting as being a very early constructional toy.

[114]

This chapter has referred again and again to the toy-making achievements of Germany, and it is pleasant to say that in one branch, toy soldiers, it was the British who exported to the Continent. The well-named William Britain made the first hollow-cast soldiers, to his own design, in 1893, using a mould made in two halves. By this technique it was easy to vary the model, and by 1907 he could offer more than a hundred different military units, as well as Zulus, circus riders and railway staff to man the model trains. Britain soldiers, with their ancillary requirements of forts, tents, guns etc., were the best available, but for a cheap army the Edwardian child could have the cut-out cardboard soldiers made in Alsace by Fischbach and Kieffer, who could produce them very inexpensively by their technique of colour printing in oil-paints.

Indeed, there were plenty of toys to be bought in Edwardian times for very little money. The Penny Bazaar could be found in every town and offered a huge range of cast metal and carved wood toys. The child with a Christmas present of five shillings could choose as many as sixty toys. Happy days!

Index

Compiled by Mrs Brenda Hall, M.A.

COUGHLAN